The Politics of the Media

JOHN WHALE

Fontana/Collins

Published by Fontana in 1977
The Politics of the Media is published in hardback by Manchester University Press.

Copyright © John Whale 1977

Made and printed in Great Britain by
William Collins Sons & Co. Ltd, Glasgow

Contents

Editors' preface

This new series aims to put into the hands of the intelligent general reader concise and authoritative accounts of the major issues of British politics today. Writing on politics has too often suffered from being either strident polemic or ephemeral journalism or else from being academic monographs too specialized and technical for the general reader. This series hopes to fill this important gap in what has been called 'the dead ground of contemporary history' (that is, it is more difficult to find reliable accounts of what happened ten or twenty years ago than fifty) by covering the issues which opinion polls and specialized opinion have judged to be the major issues of contemporary British politics. We say 'issues' deliberately and not *problems*. Perhaps, indeed, beneath all these political issues there are fundamental economic and social problems. Theories are not lacking to explain them all and to put them all in a 'correct theoretical perspective'. Our aim is more modest and precise: to remedy the lack of books that give accounts of the issues which, doubtless, reflect forces more fundamental.

Each book will cover three main topics and, ordinarily, will be in this form: (i) a brief summary of the origins of the issue and fuller account of its history since the Second World War; (ii) an account of its institutional setting and of the pressure groups associated with the issues; and (iii) an account of what should be done and what is likely to happen. We ask each author to be as objective and as balanced as is possible in the first two sections, but as polemical and as stimulating as he or she cares to or thinks fit in the third.

The series aims to achieve the same high standards of judgement but also of brevity that have been typical of the Fontana MODERN MASTERS series, that is to be intellectually demanding but completely non-technical. It aims to fulfil much the same function: both to be an intelligent and readily comprehensible introduction to the general reader and to be a way in which a specialist in one field can communicate with a specialist in another. If we may draw an analogy, we have briefed our authors to attempt that intellectually demanding but completely non-technical level of writing that is typical of the *Political Quarterly* at its best. Yet while the series is primarily intended for the educated general reader, students of history, politics, economics and social administration will find that the books fill a gap. They reflect a growing concern in the academic study of politics to look first at actual issues, rather than at institutions or methodologies.

If new editions are warranted, the first and second sections of each book will, of course, be revised. But each time there is a reprint, we will ask the author to update the third section on policy, on what is being done. Thus each reprint will be topical while the edition places the issue in a deeper historical and institutional setting. We hope that this novel feature of the series will help it to be a contribution to what Walter Bagehot once called 'the political education of mankind'. For that education seems at the moment so often to suffer from books which are a strange mixture of abstract theory and instant polemic. Issues need studying in an historical context if we are to act sensibly and effectively; but act we must.

Bernard Crick
Patrick Seyd

PART ONE

*Origins and context:
the course of the argument
since the Second World War*

Chapter 1: 1945-55

On the occasions in the past thirty years when the media have been the subject-matter of politics, the root question has been this: which sources of power within them, if any, should be backed or opposed by the ultimate power of the State?

'Media' is an unattractive term. It is foreign in form, and vague. A rocket-launched satellite can be a medium of mass communication (to spell out the singular); so can a brick wall. But the term is convenient once defined. It is used in this book as a short name for the chief dispensers of news in the United Kingdom: nationally distributed newspapers, radio and television.

Politicians are in the business of moving opinion; and most of them believe the media to be peculiarly potent tools to that end. Many journalists are not so sure. There is a good deal of evidence, academic and commonsensical, that the media do more towards corroborating opinion than creating it. People contrive to choose and sift what they read or see or hear until it fits their views. Even if journalism does not determine what people think, though, it clearly guides what they think about. Either way, the politician is understandably anxious that journalists should share his judgements about what is right, what is important. He is regularly disappointed. So he is often tempted to urge Government-induced changes in the control of the media, with the hope of bringing journalists round.

Governments have had no formal hold over newspapers in this country since 1695, when Puritan and Stuart censorship was renounced under William III and the Licensing Act was not renewed. Indirect controls lasted till 1855, when Palmerston's first administration repealed the Newspaper Stamp Duties Act: the stamp had been a special postage rate which newspapers had had to pay, whether they were to be sent by post or not, and it had therefore operated against the founding both of provincial papers (swamped by competition from London through the mails) and of papers which working people could afford. That gone, newspapers offered the State no handle. They depended on no favour it could bestow or withhold.

Broadcasting, on the other hand, has been open to Government manipulation from the beginning. The difference is that the number of possible newspapers is infinite; the number of available cable or wireless channels is finite. As early as the Electric Telegraph Act 1863, the principle was laid down that the State had the right to commandeer a scarce means of communication at need. When the British Broadcasting Company (later Corporation) began radio transmissions in 1922, and when it was joined in 1955 by commercial television and in 1972 by commercial radio, the law was each time made clear: ministers could tell the BBC and the Independent Broadcasting Authority (which had charge of all commercial broadcasting) to broadcast or withhold whatever the Government wanted.

That particular cannon has seldom been fired. It is not much use to party politicians: it was meant to guard the interests of the State (especially in wartime), not of any one political party. It is true that politicians are prone to see their party's interests and the State's as the same; but for as long as the United Kingdom avoids one-party rule, most politicians perceive that the group which deploys the power of the State against a rival may find itself repaid in the same coin. 'Do as you would be done by' has seemed a prudent maxim.

So politicians have had to look for indirect ways of bringing State power to bear on unsympathetic journalism, broadcast as well as printed. Their chief effort has gone into drafting new rules for the way the media are to be owned and run. The aim has been not to control the media, or even to control the controllers, but to determine the kind of people who may acquire control. In this struggle, the main target for politicians has been concentration of ownership. Nothing alarms them more than to see control of the media in only a few hands. The reason is plain enough. If (to take common charges) newspapers and broadcasting represent capitalist values, or if on the other hand the people who actually take the editorial decisions in both are disrespectful radicals, then the problem is all the greater as the number of different managements is fewer. The chance of the saving exception is reduced.

That feeling, shared by Labour and Conservatives, has been the main drive behind the three pairs of Government-instigated inquiries which provide the framework for the story of relations between politicians and the media since the Second World War. There has been Ross on the press and Beveridge on broadcasting, in the late 1940s; Shawcross and Pilkington, in the early 1960s; McGregor and Annan, in the middle 1970s. You might have expected this particular weapon to be trained more often on broadcasting than on newspapers. Broadcasting was unarguably a monopoly until 1955, and control was still concentrated after that. Besides, the BBC's Charter from the Government has never been renewed for more than twelve years at a time, so that there has been recurrent occasion to look quizzically at the Corporation's performance. Despite that, there have been as many postwar inquiries into the press as into broadcasting; and indeed Ross on the press was the first of the whole series.

The appointment of a Royal Commission on the Press under Sir David Ross, the retiring head of an Oxford college, followed directly from an October 1946 debate on the press in the Commons. The debate can well stand as a specimen of many disputes before and since; and in the course of it, the arguments proceeding from concentration were paramount. On this occasion the members who put them were all Labour: the motion for debate – it asked for a Royal Commission because of 'increasing public concern

13

at the growth of monopolistic tendencies in the control of the press and with the object of furthering the free expression of opinion' – stood in the name of six Labour backbenchers. One of them, Haydn Davies, explained that the motion grew out of a resolution at that year's conference of the National Union of Journalists, of which he was a member. He explained (*Commons Hansard*, 29 October 1946):

> We claim that, from the inside, we know more about the freedom of the press than anybody else. For years we have watched this freedom being whittled away. We have watched the destruction of great papers. We have watched the combines come in, buying up and killing independent journals, and we have seen the honourable profession of journalism degraded by high finance and big business. Worst of all, as a result of this, we have watched subservience replace judgement, and we are worried.

It was well understood that big business had common interests with the Conservative party. The motion was seconded by Michael Foot, then a young Labour member who had been in the House only a year. His chief target was Lord Kemsley, the owner of a string of newspapers in London and outside. Within thirteen years the Kemsley papers were sold and their political colour variegated; but in the 1945 election which had brought Labour to power they had been a mainstay of the Conservative campaign. Foot said:

> I am not denying the right of Lord Kemsley, if he wishes, to distort the news. I do not think it is possible to devise a law to stop Lord Kemsley from distorting the news which would not also interfere with the legitimate rights of other and reputable newspaper proprietors. But what I do deny is the right of Lord Kemsley to distort the news not only in London but in Aberdeen, Cardiff, Bristol and other cities. If the news is to be distorted in places like

Aberdeen, I should think the people of Aberdeen could find someone to do it for themselves. There is no case whatever on grounds of freedom why chain newspapers should be allowed to exist. These chain newspapers have not been built up by the choice of the public. They have been built up by financial manipulation. Therefore I say that the main purpose of this Royal Commission should be to inquire into the operation of chain news-papers, and to devise a law to prevent the spreading of these chain newspapers, and to break up the chains that already exist.

In the same spirit, the chief defence of the prevailing system of ownership came from a senior Conservative, Sir David Maxwell Fyfe. The use of the term 'monopoly', he submitted, was an abuse of words where readers had such variety of choice. The London morning papers were divided between seven independent groups; those supporting the Government sold roughly as many copies each day as the pro-Conservative ones; more than half the provincial dailies were independent, and the remainder were divided between four groups of owners. Maxwell Fyfe drew this inference:

What is really wanted, and what is behind this motion, is not freedom of expression at all. Honourable members want to saddle the country with a number of papers of their own way of thinking.

Herbert Morrison, for the Government, nevertheless found that the case for an inquiry was made out, and a Royal Commission was duly appointed the following April. Its charge was 'to inquire into the control, management and ownership of the newspaper and periodical press and the news agencies, including the financial structure and the monopolistic tendencies in control, and to make recom-mendations thereon'. The Commission worked for two years, and in the end produced an answer which was a rebuke to the ideologues of both sides.

There was nothing approaching monopoly in the press as a whole, the Commission concluded (report, June 1949, cmnd 7700, pars. 664–79). The largest single group, Kemsley's, owned seventeen per cent of daily and Sunday papers, and twenty-four per cent of provincial morning papers. In fifty-eight towns out of sixty-six in Britain where daily newspapers were published there was a local monopoly; but its importance was qualified by the fact that national newspapers circulated throughout the country. Between 1921 and 1948 there had been a marked tendency away from concentration of ownership in the national press, and in the provinces there was no reason to expect much increase in it. The present degree of concentration was not so great as to prejudice the free expression of opinion or the accurate presentation of news.

Nevertheless, the Commission went on, in point of truthfulness and balance 'all the popular papers and certain of the quality fall short of the standard achieved by the best, either through excessive partisanship or through distortion for the sake of news value'. But the causes of these shortcomings did not lie in any particular form of ownership; and here came the key passage (par. 680):

The press is part of our political machinery, which is essentially partisan, and it is a highly competitive industry, the principle of whose being is to maintain high circulations. The increasing complexity of public affairs and the growth of the reading public have created a need for public instruction on an entirely new scale, without producing as yet either the corresponding demand or the corresponding supply. The failure of the press to keep pace with the requirements of society is attributable largely to the plain fact that an industry that lives by the sale of its products must give the public what the public will buy. A newspaper cannot, therefore, raise its standard far above that of its public and may anticipate profit from lowering its standard in order to gain an advantage over a competitor. This tendency is not always resisted as firmly as the public interest requires.

In other words, the fault was in human nature, abetted by the known competitiveness of newspapermen. Since the reform of human nature lay outside the Commission's reach, it recommended instead an attempt at reforming the behaviour of newspapermen. They were to take on the task themselves, through a General Council of the Press. The Council would be partly made up of journalists and partly not, and among its main objects should be (par. 662) 'to encourage the growth of the sense of public responsibility and public service among all engaged in the profession of journalism'. None of the State's power would be vested in it: it would build up a code by censuring undesirable types of journalistic conduct, and would depend for its effectiveness on moral authority and nothing more.

Even that modest proposal ran into trouble. Two former journalists on the Commission were uneasy about the Council's containing members who were not journalists. The newspaper industry was unenthusiastic: it felt itself largely vindicated by the Commission's report, and it feared restriction. Four years went by before slow deliberations among newspapermen produced a Council – without non-journalist members; and in between there had been pressure from the NUJ, reproachful letters in *The Times* from members of the defunct Commission, and a backbench attempt at legislation in the Commons. The Council's first pronouncement (in July 1953) was to declare it 'contrary to the best traditions of British journalism' that the *Daily Mirror* should have run a poll of its readers on whether Princess Margaret should marry her father's equerry, Group-Captain Peter Townsend.

The story of the Ross Commission is parallelled by the story of the Beveridge Committee on broadcasting, which

17

began work in the month Ross reported. It was set up (under Lord Beveridge, also a former Oxford college head) in the same atmosphere of resentment at concentrated control. No other body but the BBC was licensed to broadcast from within the United Kingdom (though broadcasts in English came into the country from Radio Luxembourg). The difference this time was that the chief scourges of monopoly were Conservatives: they believed much more fervently than Labour did that the BBC was against them. Beveridge was also like Ross in that its principal consequence was largely unforeseen at the beginning. But because the State had already made itself the chief umpire of broadcasting in a way it had long since ceased to be of newspaper publishing, and the decisions which had to follow from Beveridge were therefore about matters of substance, that unpremeditated product was something bigger than just a regulatory council. It was a complete alternative system of broadcasting.

At the end of the Second World War, in 1945, nothing seemed less likely. The BBC's repute stood as high as any national institution's ever has. For more than twenty years, despite its theoretical subordination to the Government, it had in practice contrived to keep itself separate in the public mind from the everyday expediencies of politics. Partly this followed from the clear sense of moral responsibility which it derived from its first Director-General, Sir John Reith – its evident anxiety to supply programmes which the whole nation could find acceptable, and yet its determination to aim for the upper rather than the lower reaches of popular taste. Partly, though, the BBC's inviolate condition was a consequence of its not having put itself in the way of being violated. During the 1926 General Strike, for example, it had resisted the wish of Winston Churchill (then Chancellor of the Exchequer) and of others in the Cabinet's Strike Committee that the BBC should be commandeered for official broadcasting – a move the Government was entitled to make; and Churchill thought the BBC's careful balance in its makeshift news bulletins was an attempt to be impartial 'between the fire and the fire-brigade'. But Reith defined it, more accurately, as an impartiality on the side of the Government; and he would put no Labour or trade union speaker on the air until after the strike. The BBC's fair-mindedness, enjoined by law, was never reckless.

The BBC had another dispute with Churchill in 1929, when he was out of office and wanted to buy broadcast time to air his divergences from his party leader, Stanley Baldwin. Reith would not let him. In general, though, the BBC's political tussles in those pre-war years were decorous; and it remained circumspect in its use of the increased prestige which war brought it. It had been developing a news service of its own since 1934, and was slowly leaving behind its dependence on news agencies. Yet it never cared as a news organization to distance itself from Government too markedly. Its news readers read the Air Ministry's claims about German aircraft shot down in the Battle of Britain without the least quaver of scepticism in their voices. No contributor could venture the kind of criticism of the Government's conduct of the war which the *Daily Mirror* dealt in. The BBC preserved its independence by dint of testing it as seldom as possible.

The most striking monument to the BBC's pliability in the immediate postwar period was the Fourteen-Day Rule. It laid down that if an issue was to be debated in Parliament within the coming fortnight, or was covered in a Bill then before either House, the BBC must not broadcast any discussion of it. Since the number of subjects thus embargoed could run into hundreds, and since parliamentary business is ordinarily known only a week in advance, it was an extremely irksome ban. Even more remarkable, it was devised by the BBC itself. The BBC governors invented it in 1944 as a talisman against ministers who wanted to make political broadcasts which colleagues in the disintegrating wartime Coalition might not approve of. But politicians delighted

19

in the rule. It fed the House of Commons's collective vanity as the nation's sole significant forum of debate. After the war the rule was formalized in an 'aide-memoire' about political broadcasting agreed between the BBC, the Government and the Opposition; and BBC officials then allowed it to stretch beyond ministerial broadcasts to political broadcasts as a whole. When the BBC realized what it had given away, its attempts at recovery were easily rebuffed. At this juncture Lord Beveridge was appointed.

His Committee reported only eighteen months later, in January 1951 (*Report of the Broadcasting Committee, 1949*, cmnd 8116). It concluded (par. 183) that 'the achievement of broadcasting in Britain is something of which any country might be proud'. Even so, the BBC needed guarding against the dangers of monopoly – dangers of size, of Londonization, of remoteness, of self-satisfaction, of secretiveness, of slowness in exploring new techniques, of favouritism and injustice in treatment of staff or performers, of a sense of divine right. But that could be most economically done by decentralization, not dismemberment. For engineering reasons there could only be a handful of broadcasting organizations, and they would all have to obey rules in the way the BBC did (pars. 171–80):

> The practical issue reduces itself to the choice between chartering three or four Broadcasting Corporations on terms requiring them to co-operate and accept Government vetoes and directions on certain points, and chartering a single Broadcasting Corporation subject to the same vetoes and requiring it to make steady progress towards greater decentralization, devolution and diversity. We have no hesitation in choosing the second of these alternatives.
>
> We make this choice, first and foremost, because we believe this is the best way of securing the flexible decentralization that we desire . . . We make this choice, second, because enforcement of the necessary conditions

of impartiality, fair treatment of minorities, regard to
national interest and regard to outside opinion, is likely
to prove easier with one Corporation than with three or
four Corporations . . . The problem as it presents itself
to us is that of devising internal as well as public and
external safeguards against misuse of broadcasting
power.

So the Committee recommended that the BBC should work
towards establishing local stations, that there should be
separate broadcasting commissions for Scotland, Wales and
Northern Ireland, that the BBC should undergo regular
parliamentary scrutiny, that the powers of the BBC's
governors should be increased, and a good deal more –
all as a way of keeping monopoly wholesome. On the other
main question, how broadcasting should be paid for, the
Committee ruled in favour of the prevailing system of
licence fees and against advertisements (par. 195):

If the people of any country want broadcasting for its
own sake they must be prepared to pay for it as listeners or viewers; they must not ask for it for nothing
as an accompaniment of advertising some other com-
modity.

Yet within four years both of those recommendations had
been flouted. The BBC's monopoly had been breached, and
by a system which was financed by advertisements.

The BBC had bad luck. It was unlucky, first, that the
voice of dissent on the Beveridge Committee came from a
Conservative politician, Selwyn Lloyd. He was already a
persuasive figure: he went on to hold two senior ministries
and the Speakership of the Commons. He was one of only
four members of the Committee who went to look at and
listen to American broadcasting. He liked the commercial
system which he saw there; and when he wrote a minority
report which suggested setting up a similar system in the

United Kingdom alongside the BBC, it gave heart and respectability to a rising group of Conservative politicians who wanted the same thing. They believed in a high-consumption society: a people emerging from the pinched aftermath of war ought to want it, advertising on television would promote it. (There was for the time no great interest in commercial radio.) Some of them were advertising men themselves. Lloyd even supplied them with a euphemism to replace awkward phrases like 'commercial' or 'advertisement-financed': *independent* competition, he said, would be healthy for broadcasting.

None of that would have mattered if the Conservatives had remained in opposition. But that was the BBC's second misfortune: two successive Governments under Clement Attlee delayed action on broadcasting for so long that in the end Attlee went out of office with the BBC's future still not settled. There had been no sense of urgency about setting Beveridge up in the first place; and although the Committee worked fast, it did not report until the first Attlee Government had come to an end and the second had struggled for nearly a year with an overall parliamentary majority of only six. By then the Government was plagued with ill health, internal divisions and an Opposition which at last scented success. An official decision to renew the BBC's monopoly was not announced until July 1951. Even then there were details in the Government scheme which its own backbenchers did not like; and the decision had still not been put into effect two months later, when Attlee felt obliged to call a general election. In October the Conservatives came to power.

The BBC's third piece of ill luck was that the man at the head of the new Government, Winston Churchill, had been quarrelling intermittently with the BBC for twenty-five years. He had no special regard for commercial television, which he is said to have called a twopenny Punch and Judy show. But he was not disposed to find any television important: he never gave a television interview; and the

BBC's monopoly was certainly not the cause for which he would hold out against the new breed of Tory MPs whose election had brought him back to power.

Many of them shared his view that the BBC carried its even-handedness between opposing political factions to absurd lengths, given that one side represented the considered wisdom of all decent people and the other an unpatriotic aberration. Some such instinctive estimate of the party battle was at the back of the belief which persisted among many Conservatives that it was the BBC which had lost them the 1945 election: they could not bring themselves to accept that the volume of Labour support which came to the surface after the Second World War was genuine, not artificially induced, and that the BBC had had a duty to reflect it.

The BBC's next stroke of ill luck was that the new 1950s generation of Conservative MPs had been elected on a denationalization ticket. The party manifesto for the October 1951 election said nothing about broadcasting. But it did say:

> The attempt to impose a doctrinaire socialism upon an island which has grown great and famous by free enterprise has inflicted serious injury upon our strength and prosperity. Nationalization has proved itself a failure which has resulted in heavy losses to the taxpayer or the consumer, or both.

The document promised to stop all further nationalization, to denationalize steel, to permit the denationalization of road haulage, and to decentralize coal and rail. All of this proved unexpectedly difficult. Time went by, and nothing had been done. The new national monopolies were unbreached. Conservatives in the constituencies grew restive. Casting around for a bastion of the monopoly principle which could be stormed without too much trouble, Conservative back-benchers could see only one: the BBC. By a final mischance, its Charter and Licence (which had been continued by Labour for five years to the end of 1951 and by the Conservatives themselves for another six months) were due for renewal at the end of June 1952.

In this atmosphere, the campaign to introduce commercial broadcasting could flourish. It was led by a handful of able backbenchers, sympathetically represented in the Cabinet by Churchill's old friend Lord Woolton, and it was backed by a wide range of interests in advertising, entertainment and television engineering. In May 1952 the Government published a White Paper (cmnd 8550) which promised that the BBC would be allowed 'to continue broadly on the existing basis' – and the Charter was duly renewed for ten years from the beginning of July. But the White Paper also contained this passage (par. 7):

> The present Government have come to the conclusion that in the expanding field of television provision should be made to permit some element of competition when the calls on capital resources at present needed for purposes of greater national importance make this feasible.

That pledge – unspecific, undated, unsubmitted to the electorate – marked a turning point in the argument, and in the whole development of British broadcasting. It was at once recognized as such by Lord Reith (as he had become), the man who had been able to set the BBC off in pursuit of 'the best of everything' because it was protected from the temptations of competition by the monopoly principle. He forced a Lords debate in which he said (*Lords Hansard*, 22 May 1952):

> A principle absolutely fundamental and cherished is scheduled to be scuttled. It is the principle that matters, and it is neither here nor there that the scuttling may not take place for years. The Government are here on record to scuttle – a betrayal and a surrender; that is what is

so shocking and serious; so unnecessary and wrong. Somebody introduced dog-racing into England . . . And somebody introduced Christianity and printing and the uses of electricity. And somebody introduced small-pox, bubonic plague and the Black Death. Somebody is minded now to introduce sponsored broadcasting into this country.

Yet by reserving the full fire of his wrath for 'sponsored' broadcasting, Reith helped to distract the debate from the main point, which was the effect on the quality of pro-grammes of competition for large audiences. Sponsored broadcasting was the system then largely prevailing in the United States, whereby advertisers provided the programmes as well as the advertisements which punctuated them. This system became the chief dread of those who opposed commercial broadcasting: they were afraid that programmes would be distorted by the advertisers themselves (as when a reference to Nazi gas chambers was suppressed by the American Gas Company). So the Government scored a considerable debating success when it put forward, in a November 1953 White Paper (cmnd 9005), a scheme for television under which advertisers would supply only the advertisements, while the programmes were made by programme companies under the eye of a Government-appointed authority (par. 7):

The Government has come to the conclusion that it is desirable to strengthen the controlling powers of such a body by making it a *public corporation*, which would own and operate the transmitting stations and other suitable fixed assets (renting from the Post Office any necessary connecting links between stations) and would hire its facilities to privately financed companies who would provide programmes and draw revenue from advertisements.

The distinction between that and sponsorship was unreal. Sponsoring later became rare in American television practice, and the indirect influence of advertisers did not diminish. Advertisers want their spots to be broadcast close to programmes which a lot of people watch. A dearth of such programmes will bring on a dearth of advertisement revenue. In any system of commercial broadcasting, therefore, sponsored or not, programme makers see good reason to make programmes which will be widely watched. The fact that the *News of the World* has for decades been the best-selling British newspaper is evidence that big audiences are not compiled by appealing to man's loftiest instincts. The American trade paper *Broadcasting* showed clearsightedness (as well as the glee which those who have lost their innocence can hardly help feeling at the sight of other people losing theirs) when it wrote of the White Paper:

> Dear little John Bulls,
> Don't you cry;
> You'll be full commercial
> Bye and bye.

Full commercial: the phrase was well judged. Once the commercial principle was established, the BBC too was altered. Its revenues still came from licence fees. But they could be increased, in an era of inflation and rapid technical change, only with Government consent. Governments were always reluctant to give that consent, because part of the odium of the move rubbed off on them. The less the BBC was watched, the more easily could consent be refused. That danger was greatly increased by the coming of a rival channel. So it became a main aim of BBC policy to have as many viewers as its rival.

It could have been fairly argued in favour of commercial television that for as long as the BBC was a monopoly it was mainly middle-class. Politically, that hardly entered the equation. It was from the middle classes that the opponents of monopoly largely came; and Labour MPs, whose working-class electors were soon watching little else than commercial television, were so sternly opposed to the Bill introducing it that the Government had to limit debate with a guillotine motion.

The Television Act, establishing commercial television under an Independent Television Authority, became law in July 1954. Well before the new programme companies (each of them regionally based) went on the air in September 1955, the BBC began to adjust its programmes to the new need. Some of these adjustments were for the better: its news bulletins introduced film in place of the still photograph of Big Ben which had been till 1954 their only illustration. Some of the changes would have come about anyway: it was in the later 1950s that the old certainties among the English middle classes about what exactly constituted 'the best of everything' – in dress, accent, music, writing, behaviour, belief – began perceptibly to fade, and the process accelerated in the 1960s. Some adjustments were resisted; and the effect was to encourage commercial broadcasters to show more interest in excellence than they otherwise might have done. The fact remained that the BBC was at last obliged to bend to public taste as it was, not as it might be; and a force for nudging standards of judgement upwards was lost.

So the Beveridge report was rejected. Its advice was ignored even on another matter it had to consider, the Fourteen-Day Rule. The Committee had been in no doubt that the ban ought to go (par. 264):

We do not see why the British democracy should not be allowed to have microphone debate of a political issue at the time when debate is most topical and interesting, that is to say when the issue is actually before Parliament. This would both increase popular interest in Parliament and popular capacity to judge the wisdom of Parliament.

27

Both these things are gains from the point of view of good democratic government.

Parliament did not think so. Between 1953 and 1955 the BBC made a number of attempts to slip out of the net it had itself woven. The party managers would not let it. The Postmaster-General turned the rule into a Government directive. Neither Churchill's departure from the premiership (in April 1955) nor the start of commercial television made any difference: in November 1955 the rule was debated in the Commons, and upheld on a free vote by 271 votes to 126. It was the last fling of the notion that broadcasters would always remain contentedly subordinate to politicians.

Chapter 2: 1955-66

Once there was competition in broadcasting, the broadcasters became more of a thorn in the side of Government than they had been before. Competition could not be confined to the pursuit of big audiences for programmes of entertainment. It necessarily extended to news programmes. A news organization working on its own can swallow uninformative explanations of official or commercial blunders, and even the refusal to explain them at all, without any great discomfort. But the moment there are rivals in its field it is afraid of appearing more gullible, less enterprising than them, lest its audience diminish.

This is swiftly translated into human terms. The number of television viewers who watch news bulletins on different channels on the same evening, and are therefore in a position to compare performance, is proportionately very small. But it includes the administrators of television news programmes. If the key interview has been secured, the key question put, on one channel but not on another, then the board of the momentarily less successful concern may ask the editor, the editor may ask the news editor, the news editor may ask the reporter, why not. All the people in that sequence will be anxious to forestall that question by showing the kind of comprehensive zeal which insures them against all risks. Part of their motive will be pride in being thought to do good work; part, and not the least part, anxiety to hold a valued job. So the most basic of economic fears helps to make competitive news-broadcasting a much more thrusting and troublesome creature than non-competitive.

The change was the more swiftly felt because Independent Television News (the organization supplying national and foreign news to all the Independent Television programme companies) made a cult of comparative irreverence from the first. Whether the matter in hand was popular music or the balance of trade, the interviewer was the respondent's cheerful adversary, putting the questions which would rise in the mind of the sceptical outsider. That had not been the BBC's way. Its practice had been much more to choose what should be held up for respect, and hold it up; and the works and words of Governments had fallen for the most part into that category. Now it was obliged to adapt itself to the new pattern of wide and yet quizzical coverage.

Alongside that, and in conflict with it, ran a new sensitivity to Government opinion. The BBC had lost a great battle; it had to make sure that it lost no more. In particular it had to ensure that Governments would allow its licence fee to go on rising, even though its likely audience had been halved.

The first notable response from the BBC to these divergent pulls was the decision to cover the 1955 round of the political party conferences, held each year in the autumn and not previously thought fit fodder for BBC cameras. ITN, then in its first month of broadcasting, declined the challenge and began its conference coverage a season later. At that period both sides used sixteen-millimetre film cameras only; but in later years the conferences became one of the main theatres of technological competition between the two sides, with more and more complicated hardware sprouting beside dank halls in windswept seaside towns. For both sides, it was an odd preoccupation. The party conferences were not news, and not important. The views voiced at them had a fearful predictability, and were indeed freely predicted in the newspapers. The decisions taken were without effect. The Conservatives, in power then and for the next nine years, had no tradition of taking any notice at all of their party conference in forming policy. In the Labour party, the primacy of conference is a recurrent cry; but it had been effectively stifled in the 1940s by Clement Attlee, and hardly reappeared until the 1970s. To suggest that Liberal party assemblies could at that time have any influence on events was pure courtesy. Yet the BBC wrote them all as immutably into the calendar of the political year as the Queen's Speech or the Budget.

One of the BBC's main motives, in which it was joined by ITV, was the ambition to televise the House of Commons. In the Commons chamber the political argument was dramatized – given personality, conflict, tension – in just the way television needed. Yet Parliament would not let the cameras in. Even still cameras and tape recorders were excluded. The only tolerated medium was the written word. The arguments used for dismissing television's claims were that it would be intrusive, meddlesome and unfair – that it would rig up towers of bright lights, encourage clowns and show pictures of members asleep. Television chiefs needed to demonstrate that these fears were groundless. The only test-bed to hand was the party conferences.

The other persuasion was the wish to win the favour of politicians, both those who now held power and those who might one day succeed to it. The conference cameras were a signal from broadcasters to ministers and potential ministers in some such terms as this: 'We are not as frivolous as we sometimes have to look. We know that politics matters. Here we are, publicly witnessing to that truth. All we ask in return is that you should not be obstructive about our revenue.'

As a manœuvre, it was as unsuccessful as it deserved to be. Politicians could see that the interest in politics was insincere: knowledgeable interest would have kept television away. Ministers were often positively irritated by the attention. It advertised the divisions in the governing party, and gave prominence to dissidents. Party conference coverage became a source of constant friction between broadcasters and rulers. Added to that, it was expensive; it bored the viewers; and it did not even have any effect on the argument about televising Parliament. (Broadcasters quickly forgot it had ever been meant to: the equipment became intrusive to the point where people sitting on the platform wore dark glasses against the fierce lights.) Yet once begun it had to go on. If it was important in 1955, it was important ever afterwards.

Like it or not, the BBC had passed out of the era when its normal relation with Government could be harmony. Such a state needs widespread agreement on the nation's aims and values, and a general sense that the Government is honouring them. A news organization speaking to and for the whole country can then confine criticism of the authorities to minor matters. If that degree of unity ever existed, it was reached only during the Second World War. Thereafter national divisions multiplied.

Nothing illustrated them more sharply than the Franco-British invasion of Suez in November 1956. To some people (including the Prime Minister, Sir Anthony Eden) Suez was an exercise in facing the dictators once again, with Colonel Nasser of Egypt as the new Hitler; to others (and to the American Government) it was a post-imperial spasm best brought to a quick end. The affair was difficult enough even for newspapers, whose audiences are each only a part of the whole nation and likely to have certain judgements in common. It was far more difficult for the BBC, feeling obliged to reflect the sharp divide in national opinion, and yet well aware of the charge that by disclosing dissent it was lessening the nation's will to persist in a task to which, through its Government, it had set its hand. Particular difficulties arose over the BBC's radio broadcasts overseas. Alerted by British diplomats stationed in the Middle East, ministers thought it outrageous that press reviews reporting damning opinions on the whole enterprise should be broadcast where British troops waiting to go into battle could hear them.

Eden told his Lord Chancellor (Maxwell Fyfe, by then Lord Kilmuir) to prepare an instrument which would bring the BBC wholly within the Government's control. It was an acknowledgement that the theoretically dictatorial powers which the Government possessed over the broadcasters did not in practice amount to very much. The practical obstacle would be the same, with or without extra powers: that the Government would still be dependent on the BBC's staff – engineers even more than journalists – to run the service, and the staff would not be prepared to put out plain Government propaganda. The Eden plan was not pressed.

The following month Eden allowed the BBC another victory. The Fourteen-Day Rule collapsed. The motion which had perpetuated it the year before had also established a Commons Select Committee to look into the rule's working and effects. The Committee had recommended that the fourteen days be reduced to seven, and that the embargo should cease to apply at all after a Bill had survived its general discussion on second reading. On those terms, the sanctity of parliamentary debate was already breached. A number of journalists and broadcasting politicians pressed for the rule's total abolition. In December 1956 Eden announced its trial suspension, and six months later it was suspended indefinitely.

Television was now becoming a mass medium. The latter half of the 1950s was its period of fastest growth. In March 1955 the number of television licences issued stood at $4\frac{1}{2}$ million: by March 1958 the figure was 8 million. That was a little less than half the total at which licences levelled off in the 1970s, but it already meant that there was at least one set to every six people in the land. Yet the medium was still new, and to many people alarming. Politicians were chiefly disquieted at the notion that political habits might change. Arm's-length representative democracy appeared in danger of giving way to something altogether more direct. In order to cover the news, television needed it turned into pictures: ideally, moving pictures. An old political form, the protest march, took on a new significance. It was an idea turned into pictures, and the pictures moved. Political lobbyists and television news editors recognized a common interest. The forces of dissent seemed suddenly to have found a new and powerful ally.

The first major beneficiary was the Campaign for Nuclear Disarmament, which in 1958 arranged an Easter march from Trafalgar Square in London to the Atomic Weapons Research Establishment at Aldermaston in Berkshire. (In later years the direction was reversed.) The march was massively covered on television, and in each of the next few years it grew in size. It had in the end absolutely no effect. The United Kingdom gradually and unacknowledgedly ceased to be an independent nuclear power as the game became too expensive, not as the domestic political climate became too hot. But for years the Aldermaston march, and the kind of people who were seen going on it, ranked as a powerful symbol of political menace or hope.

While television was in this way altering the techniques of politics from outside, it was also busy within the gates. The caution of the BBC in its television coverage of politics until the late 1950s had not been all timidity. Elections, in particular, held a special interest for television, because of the conflict and tension they represented; but they held a special danger, too. For decades there had been a legal limit to the amount of money which might be spent in presenting any one candidate to the electorate. But journalistic coverage did that, and cost a great deal of money. The 1949 Representation of the People Act had exempted newspapers, but (by a remarkable omission) not broadcasting. The simplest act of broadcast reporting might be held a breach of the law.

The paralysis which this induced in the BBC – as late as the general election of May 1955 no campaign speeches were quoted on its television news bulletins – could not long survive the coming of ITV. The law itself was not tested in the courts till after the October 1964 election, when Sir Alec Douglas-Home's local Communist opponent (the Scottish poet Hugh McDiarmid) unsuccessfully claimed that the television time bestowed on Sir Alec as Conservative leader meant that he had broken the law as Conservative candidate in Kinross and West Perthshire; and the Act was not amended to exempt broadcasting as well as newspapers till 1969. But as early as February 1958 an ITV programme company, Granada, broadcast all three candidates in a by-election at Rochdale. In the general election of October 1959 television began to show what it could do. Speeches were quoted, debates mounted. The party organizations, for their part, made great efforts towards the sophisticated filling of the allowance of free broadcast time which was theirs by law. Many politicians believed that all this portended profound change. Perhaps they would have been a little comforted if they had known that when the party broadcasts went out – they were carried simultaneously on both channels – a fifth of the entire audience switched off its sets.

At the same time, equally troubling shifts of power could be detected in the world of newspapers. Here the harbinger of change was Roy Thomson, the Canadian owner of a number of newspapers and broadcasting stations in smallish North American towns. In September 1953, a man of fifty-nine looking for a new interest after the death of his wife, he had taken his opportunity and bought the *Scotsman*, an old-established morning paper published in Edinburgh. In May 1955, partly on the strength of this new dignity, he had been awarded the franchise to run Scottish Television, the principal ITV company in Scotland. Now, in August 1959, the rapidly increasing value of his television holding enabled him to buy Kemsley Newspapers – regional morning papers in seven important cities from Aberdeen to Cardiff, and a few national Sunday papers, including the *Sunday Times*. (Kemsley himself, the owner till then, had been worried by falling income and the prospect of heavy death duties.)

Thomson proved in time to be a remarkably light-handed proprietor, with even a touch of the soft-heartedness which newspapers sometimes bring out in the hardest-headed tycoons. But he had something of the New World's irreverence for the solemnities of the Old, and it was his simple pleasure to talk as if nothing interested him about newspapers or broadcasting except the making of money. His success could therefore be taken as evidence that the world of newspapers was run on the principles of the jungle, where the strong triumphed and the weak perished.

That impression was reinforced during 1960, when two minor Sunday papers in the Kemsley group – the *Sunday Graphic* in London and the *Empire News* in Manchester – disappeared in a Thomson reorganization. But the chief confirmation seemed to come from an event which had nothing to do with Thomson: the closure in October 1960 of the *News Chronicle*. With it went one of the three London evening papers, the *Star* (whose chief distinction was that it had once employed George Bernard Shaw as music critic). Three months later, financial troubles came to a head at Odhams, a magazine empire which owned the *Daily Herald* and the *Sunday People*. Here Thomson was again implicated. He was offered Odhams; the possibility of his getting it prompted a counter-bid, and in February 1961 the prize passed to the Mirror Group. The *Daily Mirror* and the *Herald* were to a large extent interested in the same readers – working-class Labour sympathizers; and although Cecil King, the Mirror Group's chairman, promised to keep the *Herald* going for a set period of years, there was not much optimism about its future in the long term.

Until the collapse of the *Chronicle*, postwar newspaper closures had not been especially alarming. It is possible to argue that the death of any newspaper diminishes newspapers in general, since the pool of journalistic talent and the opportunity for developing it are thereby lessened. Considered for themselves, though, the newspapers which folded in the 1950s were undistinguished and unlamented. (The only national newspaper among them was the *Sunday Chronicle*.) The rate of closure had been at least as fast, and more damaging, in the 1920s, when the *Pall Mall*

Gazette had been absorbed by the *Evening Standard*, when the *Westminster Gazette* had been swallowed by the *Daily News* (which had had Dickens as its first editor) and then the *Daily News* merged into the *News Chronicle*, and when the number of towns outside London with two or more morning papers fell from fifteen to eight.

But the *News Chronicle* was a special case. Not merely was it the sole survivor of a long Liberal tradition – besides the *Daily News* it had two other nineteenth-century London morning papers in its pedigree, the *Daily Chronicle* and the *Morning Leader* – but it employed a number of able writers and had the affection of the readers who bought it. (The fact that they still numbered one and a quarter million, and yet were not enough to keep the paper going, was seen as proof of the cruel absurdity of newspaper economics.) Besides that, it occupied, together with the *Herald*, a narrow ledge of middle ground between posh papers and popular, between the stately and the trivial. Both papers spoke to largely working-class audiences, but they spoke as to people who wanted serious issues seriously treated.

The double loss, and the continuing shock from the Thomson irruption into British journalism, was enough to set up a demand for a new inquiry into the state of the press. Harold Macmillan, who had succeeded Eden as Conservative Prime Minister not long after Suez, was at first resistant; but the tussle over the body of the *Herald* finally persuaded him that there was 'some general unease in the industry', and a Royal Commission was appointed. Broadcasting was only slightly differently handled. The BBC's July 1952 Charter would run out at the end of June 1962 (and was in fact extended to the end of July 1964, to synchronize it with the ITA's first ten-year stint under the 1954 Television Act). The unease among politicians about television's effects made it wise to hold an inquiry before powers were renewed; but (as with Beveridge) a committee, reporting to specific ministers rather than to the whole Government, was thought adequate.

So the second postwar pair of inquiries was set in train. The Committee on Broadcasting began work in September 1960 under Sir Harry Pilkington, a businessman; the Royal Commission on the Press in February 1961 under Lord Shawcross, a lawyer and former Labour minister.

Neither changed much; and yet both had their effect on attitudes, and even on legislation. The Shawcross report was published in September 1962 (*Royal Commission on the Press, 1961–2*, cmnd 1811). It gave a useful airing to the problem of inefficiency in newspaper offices (pars. 81–91) – the senior managers who all left the building before the presses began to turn, the 700 men employed by one popular paper to tie up bundles with string when there were string-tying machines to be had, the elderly men sent home every night on full pay after two hours' work, the presses used below the speeds for which they were designed, the one-third reduction in the wages bill which was theoretically possible; and for once newspapers could write about all this, because an outside body had brought it up. But those were not the main reasons why newspapers failed, the report said. The real killer was competition.

The slow disappearance of wartime restrictions during the 1950s had brought back 'true competition both in circulation and size' (par. 164). Among popular national papers, which were anyway losing readers to the quality papers, competition was particularly fierce both for readers and for the advertisement revenue they brought. In that struggle, the weak could only grow weaker (par. 221):

Within any class of competitive newspapers, the economies of large-scale operation provide a natural tendency for a newspaper which already has a large circulation to flourish, and to attract still more readers, whilst a newspaper which has a small circulation is likely to be in difficulties. The problem is not so much why the *News Chronicle* could not survive with a circulation of one and a quarter million, but how it could get anywhere near to surviving in competition against newspapers with a circulation of over four million.

The Commission considered (pars. 285–312) a number of schemes which would redistribute advertising revenue in order to 'mitigate the present disadvantages of those newspapers which have a smaller circulation than the average for their class'. But Lord Shawcross himself, and one of his four colleagues, regarded all the proposals as 'divorced from the political realities of a free society'; and the whole quintet scouted the idea of Government subsidy, as the Ross Commission had done thirteen years before, and found unenthusiastically in favour of the free market (par. 313):

We are all forced to the conclusion – which we regret because of our clear realization of the dangers which exist – that there is no acceptable legislative or fiscal way of regulating the competitive and economic forces so as to ensure a sufficient diversity of newspapers. The only hope of the weaker newspapers is to secure – as some have done in the past – managers and editors of such enterprise and originality as will enable these publications to overcome the economic forces affecting them.

The Commission did put forward (pars. 337–51) one palliative for the economic anxieties which had brought it to birth; and the idea was in part adopted. It was for a press amalgamations court, which should scrutinize mergers of daily or Sunday newspapers selling more than 3 million copies in aggregate, and approve the transactions only if they met certain tests of the public interest. The proposal was finally legislated after Harold Wilson's first Labour Government had come to power in 1964 (a year in which five more provincial evening papers closed down, leaving only Glasgow and London with more than one). But it had become more restrictive than the original plan. Under

39

the terms of the new Monopolies and Mergers Act, the issue was to be decided by the Government, not the courts: permission was to come from the Board of Trade, advised by a special panel of the Monopolies Commission. The circulation limit, too, was lowered from 3 million to half a million; and unapproved transfer could earn a prison sentence of up to two years. The Press Council protested unavailingly that press freedom depended on the absence of just such laws.

The Act became law in August 1965. The first newspaper case heard under it, and for many years the most important, was the merger of *The Times* with the *Sunday Times*, predominantly under the ownership of Roy Thomson (by then Lord Thomson). 'The greatest thing I had ever done', he later called it. The circulation of *The Times* had stayed at the same inadequate level for some years, during a period of economic and cultural growth when other quality newspapers were expanding fast; and its management no longer felt able to carry the burden. In return for certain assurances about the editorial independence of both papers (promises which were kept without difficulty), the Monopolies Commission and the Government approved the merger in December 1966. As it turned out, *The Times* had missed the tide: the national economy began its long recession the following year.

The Shawcross Commission's other main effort (pars. 320–6) was to extend its own usefulness by strengthening the Press Council to carry on its work. 'Full advantage has certainly not been taken of the existence of a body representing the press as a whole to enlarge public knowledge of the problems which the press have to face.' Besides concerning itself with professional standards, said the report, the Council ought to keep abreast of changes in the control of newspapers, make sure that the public was abreast too, and be ready to hear complaints from journalists about undue influence by advertisers and even proprietors. To that end, the Council ought to equip itself with the non-journalist chairman and members (about a fifth of the whole) which the Ross Commission had recommended, and to see that the newspaper owners and the journalists' unions gave it the money for the job.

It was true that the Council had been a marginal presence in its first nine years of existence since 1953. It had cleared newspaper photographers of behaving intrusively at the Munich hospital where surviving members of the Manchester United football team were being tended in February 1958 after an air crash; it had pronounced 'grossly lewd and salacious' certain accounts of the amorous adventures of Diana Dors and of Errol Flynn published during 1960 in the *News of the World*, the *Sunday Pictorial* and the *People*; and in February 1961 it declared that for the *Spectator*, the *Guardian* and the *Observer* actually to print 'certain "four-letter" words mentioned in the *Lady Chatterley's Lover* trial' for no better reason than that they had been spoken in court was 'both objectionable and unnecessary'. Perhaps conscious that this kind of thing had not been a complete response to the issues which had been convulsing the world of newspapers, the Council moved faster to comply with Shawcross's advice than it had with Ross's. Within little more than a year it had changed at least its membership and its name. From January 1964 onward it was led by a lay chairman (a retired judge, Lord Devlin), and had five lay members out of twenty-five; and it was formally called a Press Council instead of a General Council of the Press.

The comparative speed of the change was partly prompted by the fact that the year which followed the publication of the Shawcross report was as uncomfortable a period in the relations between politicians and newspapermen as there had been for many years. In March 1963 two journalists were given brief terms of imprisonment for contempt of court when they refused to disclose sources to a tribunal of inquiry. The tribunal had been set up after a whole flurry of accusations against ministers in the Macmillan Government who had been concerned with an Admiralty clerk convicted of spying, Christopher Vassall. Newspapermen took the line that the sentences were a menace to the liberty of the subject and the press; politicians were free with the contention that the journalists had refused to disclose their sources because they had very few to disclose, and that the press had got a little of what it deserved. The tribunal declared all the accusations unfounded.

Then during the summer of 1963 great parts of the press took a passionate interest in the slow discovery that the British war minister, John Profumo, had shared a mistress with a Russian naval attaché in London. The mistress's memoirs were serialized in the *News of the World* for £23,000; increasingly fantasticated tales of high-life orgies were hawked in Fleet Street, and many were believed even if they were not bought. The frenzy only died away after Harold Macmillan had given place to Sir Alec Douglas-Home as Prime Minister in October 1963. (Sir Alec lasted a year before Labour came to power.) Neither Government nor press was at its best at that time, and the memory lingered.

The Pilkington Committee on Broadcasting, which had been appointed a little ahead of the Shawcross Commission and reported before it, aimed at larger effects and missed them; but it did at least help the BBC out of a hole. The findings themselves (*Report of the Committee on Broadcasting, 1960*, cmnd 1753) were published in June 1962. The secretariat aside, the committee member who took the lead in drafting the report was Richard Hoggart, then a professor of English at Birmingham: his book *The Uses of Literacy*, published five years before, had dealt with the way in which working-class culture was being debased by mass-produced entertainment. The report did not address itself directly to politicians' concerns. The sharpest observation it made about television news was to say (par. 317): 'We think it would be better if the use of dubbed music were forgone in the presentation of items of serious news.' The report's main concern was with the nation's cultural and intellectual life. Complaints that television impoverished it were recorded with approval (pars. 101–2):

> Subjects billed as controversial sometimes avoided the controversy, and so served rather to reinforce than to disturb prejudice and complacency. Programmes which exemplified emotional tawdriness and mental timidity helped to cheapen both emotional and intellectual values. Plays or serials might not deal with real human problems, but present a candy-floss world . . . Our own conclusion is that triviality is a natural vice of television, and that where it prevails it operates to lower general standards of enjoyment and understanding.

The Committee had no difficulty in spotting the villain (par. 209). 'The disquiet about and dissatisfaction with television are, in our view, justly attributed very largely to the service of Independent Television.' Certainly that service was popular. But the delivery of large audiences to advertisers was only the second of the purposes which ITV was meant to serve. The first was good broadcasting – responsible, varied, innovative. The two objectives did not coincide (par. 569). 'The secondary objective has been realized; the first has not.'

The men who ran ITV had in part brought this judgement on themselves. Their submissions to Pilkington had been perfunctory and smug; and they had not been deferential enough to current orthodoxy about the fearsome capacity of television for moulding minds. The BBC was in no danger of making that mistake. It was also able to satisfy the Committee (p. 47) that the kinds of programme which the BBC gave more time to than ITV did included classic serials, plays, travelogues, news, topical discussion, sport and hobbies, whereas ITV's bent was towards light entertainment, crime, comedy, 'real-life' serials and westerns.

The Committee concluded that the trouble with ITV was

organic, and could be cured only by separating the making of programmes from the selling of advertising time. So the main Pilkington proposal (pars. 578–9) was that the Independent Television Authority, as the Government-appointed body meant to oversee ITV, should be vested with 'the reality of power': it should sell the advertising time and plan the programmes, and all that would be left to the programme companies would be to make them.

The proposal was greeted with a howl, or a yawn, of rage and derision. Roy Thomson, as head of Scottish Television, called it 'completely biased, socialistic and unrealistic'. Another programme company head gave a garden party to burn the report in effigy. An attempt by one or two Labour politicians to bring Labour out in Pilkington's favour came to nothing: Labour's leaders were too well aware that ITV was the channel most of their voters watched. The reaction of Conservative ministers and backbenchers was fairly shown by the Postmaster-General, Reginald Bevins, in a volume of political memoirs he published three years later (*The Greasy Pole*, p. 86):

> I myself felt at the time that the Pilkington report was unbalanced in its strictures upon commercial television and had given far too much weight to the views of the 'do-gooders' whose opinions, rather than the opinions of the public, seemed to have dominated the minds of the Pilkington Committee.

In that unwelcoming climate, the report was still-born. A few of its recommendations were put into effect. The right to party political broadcasts was extended: by the time of the October 1964 election the Welsh and the Scottish Nationalists were allowed five minutes each. Advertising magazines disappeared: Pilkington had denounced them (pars. 258–9) as 'merely strings of advertisements' which 'rely on the charm of a winning personality or a mildly dramatic situation to give them a kind of unity' and where 'the distinction insisted on by the (Television) Act – between the programme and the advertisement – is blurred'. But for the rest the ITV caravan passed on.

Yet the report had its effect. During the late 1950s the BBC had been through a bad time. It had shifted its standards perceptibly, and even so it had lost viewers to ITV by the million. It feared for its revenues, always dependent on Government readiness to maintain the purchasing power of the licence fee. It wanted a second channel, a left arm, to free its right arm to fight ITV on level terms. Pilkington now came to its aid. 'The BBC know good broadcasting', the report said (par. 149); 'by and large, they are providing it.' The Pilkington recommendation (pars. 900–7) was that the BBC should be allowed a second channel at once, but ITV only after it had been reformed.

By 1962 the BBC was already beginning to clamber out of the valley. Under Hugh Carleton Greene, who became Director-General in January 1960, it was learning that the only way to compete was to defy the public interest and run like against like. If ITV was capturing the audience in the early evening with *Emergency Ward 10*, the BBC must run at least as winsome a serial at the same time. Greene's achievement was to release the latent creativity among broadcasters which ITV had once been expected to bring forward. BBC plays became positively exploratory, in technique and morals. Space and talent were found for political satire with edge. The change disturbed a number of the BBC's traditional supporters: a Shropshire school-mistress, Mrs Mary Whitehouse, had a certain success in drawing together their protests. But it did wonders for the BBC's flagging self-confidence; and Pilkington helped in the revival.

It had been the Conservatives, at the beginning of their long period of rule between 1951 and 1964, who had thrust the BBC out into a new and painful world. It was now the Conservatives, near the end of their mandate, who supplied a little comfort. In April 1964 the Corporation was allowed to begin transmitting BBC-2. This was a long way from Reithianism regained; although comparatively high culture was at last being broadcast on television, alternatives were much more easily found than they had been in the old days of radio; but at least the new channel salved the Reithian conscience enough to let the BBC get on with competing uninhibitedly for big audiences on its main channel. Three months later the BBC Charter was extended for a further twelve years. A new Television Act became law at the same time, extending the ITA's mandate by the same span. During its passage through Parliament there were vociferous Conservative demands that the Bill should give a firm date in 1965 by which ITV-2 should be on the air. The commitment was to be a compensation for the mild levy on turnover which the Bill exacted from programme companies, then prospering hugely. Bevins, the minister in charge, held to his intentions despite a certain amount of Cabinet pressure the other way, and he came no nearer promising an ITV-2 than a verbal undertaking to 'see how things go'. The question was buried for most of the twelve-year period.

The BBC's only effective defeat, during this middle 1960s period, was shared with ITV. The Commons twice voted down the suggestion that it should be televised. The idea had been backed by politicians like Aneurin Bevan, Iain Macleod and Jo Grimond (men who could only profit from wider exposure); it was kept alive by the televising not just of party conferences but also, from 1959, of the State opening of Parliament; and there were hopes that it would finally be brought to success by the influx of new MPs when Labour came to power in October 1964. In fact a proposal for a closed-circuit experiment was voted down in May 1965; and it was defeated again, more narrowly, after a further batch of new Labour MPs had confirmed Harold Wilson's premiership in April 1966.

Essentially the argument was about means and ends. If Parliament was simply a means to representative government, one that had adapted itself to the practicalities in the past and must continue to change if it was to remain useful, then the cameras ought to come in. If Parliament was so developed and sophisticated an instrument that its preservation unaltered was an end in itself, then they ought not. For the time being, the decision was taken to conserve the immediate institution and let the ultimate objective take care of itself.

Chapter 3: 1966-76

The third postwar decade was an ill-tempered one for the United Kingdom. It was a period of steady economic decline, accompanied by falling national influence abroad and diminishing personal wealth at home. Both Government and media looked for someone to blame, and found it in each other.

Labour politicians were no natural admirers of the press. It was irredeemably capitalist without even the saving virtue of being well managed: a detailed survey completed by the Economist Intelligence Unit in November 1966 confirmed as much. The report followed and amplified Shawcross in claiming that heavy dependence on advertisements (the chief badge of the free-market economy) was even more menacing to newspapers than overmanning. Throughout the first twenty months or so of Labour rule, relations between Government and press were nevertheless preternaturally sweet. Harold Wilson was the first Prime Minister to make friends with political journalists in any numbers. They therefore became aware not just that he was an amiable man but that he was a very gifted man, with economic notions which sounded fresh and promising; and, as citizens, they very much wanted him to succeed. They admired his cleverness, and he admired their percipience in spotting it. At first, too, his tiny parliamentary majority sufficiently explained why he could not actually change anything. But once the March 1966 general election had put an end to that excuse, and the July 1966 sterling crisis had shown that the new age of miracles was not yet, disillusion carried him lower in the minds of journalists than he would ever have descended from more ordinary beginnings; and it was matched on Wilson's side by the sourness of the man who feels himself betrayed.

The sign of this was a renewed readiness on the part of

Government to invoke the machinery of the law, and sometimes even to go beyond it. In October 1966 a huge spoil-heap slid into the South Wales coal-mining village of Aberfan. It buried 144 people, most of them children. Newspapermen and broadcast journalists descended on Aberfan in great numbers; and while rescue work was still going on under arc lights in the foul black mud, they were able to accumulate a good deal of evidence that the tip had been the object of local mistrust for at least two years. The implication of murderous official incompetence was very clear.

The Chairman of the National Coal Board, Lord Robens, affected to miss the point by criticizing much of this reporting as making a spectacle of private grief. The Government acted more directly. Two days after appointing a tribunal of inquiry, it sought to deter journalists from further interviews or comment by threatening them (through the Attorney-General, Sir Elwyn Jones) with actions for contempt of court.

It was a clear attempt to extend, by ministerial pronouncement, a law which the press already found uncertain and obstructive. The tribunal was not a trial, parallel press researches might help it, and since there would be no jury there was little danger of improper influence. The Leader of the Opposition, the Press Council and various journalistic bodies all protested. The move had at any rate the effect of shifting press indignation to a safe target, the Attorney-General.

The issue he had raised remained unsettled. It so happened that a Royal Commission on Tribunals of Inquiry had just finished its report, which was published a month later. After an interval its chairman, Lord Justice Salmon, undertook a second inquiry into the specific point about contempt. In June 1969 he recommended (cmnd 4078) that it should not be a contempt to comment on the subject-matter of a tribunal, but only to interview or report in a way which might colour tribunal evidence. Four years later the two sets of Salmon findings were referred to a new inquiry into contempt. The law's delays can be as nothing to the delays of politicians dealing with the law. (The lingering legal issues which arose in such plenty during the late 1960s and early 1970s are considered in chapter 8 of this book. Cross-references can be found from the index.)

The hand of Harold Wilson was more directly visible in the D notice affair. D (for defence) notices are warnings to editors, from an official committee on which they are represented, that mention of some specific item might contravene the Official Secrets Acts. One morning in February 1967 the lead story in the *Daily Express* was an account of the way the Government scrutinized private international cables. Instead of confining himself to saying that the system had been in force for forty years, Wilson was so incensed by the suggestion of Labour snooping that he alleged the story to be 'a clear breach of two D notices' and even – at a later stage – a danger to life. The press and the Opposition believed that Wilson was again shielding maladministration, this time by invoking the safety of the realm. A committee of Privy Councillors was set up to investigate. It concluded that there had been no breach. Wilson rejected the finding, and at the same time endeared himself to nobody by implying that he had been badly served by various officials. Both he and the newspapers showed themselves over-sensitive to criticism. In his volume of memoirs called *The Labour Government 1964–1970* (Weidenfeld/Michael Joseph, 1971), Wilson accurately recaptures (p. 418) the dyspepsia of those days of mutual disappointment:

> I was wrong to make an issue of it in the first instance. It was a very long time before my relations with the press were repaired, and I was entering upon a period when I needed justice at least, if mercy was too much to expect. I had neither.

Labour opinion as a whole was already being confirmed in its despondent view of the press by the story of the *Daily Herald*. When Cecil King bought it for the Mirror Group in 1961, he had promised to keep it going for seven years. That purchase had already marked the end of the *Herald* as a Labour newspaper: the shareholding in it of the Trades Union Congress and Labour's National Executive, 100 per cent in 1922, declined to 49 per cent when the paper had to seek help from Odhams in 1929 and then to nothing in 1961. King behaved honourably by the *Herald*, but he could hardly be expected to make it an effective competitor with his own *Mirror*. Its reappearance in 1964 as the *Sun*, with the Herald's old near-broadsheet shape and most of its old features, made very little difference to its finances. It lost money unremittingly. By the spring of 1969 it had lost over £12 million; but at least the seven-year pledge was fulfilled, with a year over. Its owners (by then called the International Publishing Corporation, and later Reed International) decided to close the paper. Robert Maxwell, a Labour MP with publishing interests, failed in an attempt to take it on as a committed Labour journal; and in the end – by a miscalculation which nevertheless seemed the only course at the time – the *Mirror* men let the *Sun* pass at a knockdown figure to Rupert Murdoch, the Australian newspaper owner who had lately bought the *News of the World*. In November 1969 Murdoch relaunched it as a tabloid which took readers from the *Mirror* from the first.

To Labour people, it was a parable of the way the economics of the newspaper industry were stacked against their side. Their rage would have been the greater if they could have foreseen the end of the story. By February 1974 the *Sun* was urging a Conservative vote.

The disputable judgement shown on both sides over Aberfan and the D notices was reproduced in the *Sunday Telegraph* secrets case. In January 1970, just at the point in the Nigerian civil war when the federal forces whom the British were backing had at any rate won, the *Sunday*

51

Telegraph published a private report by a British diplomat which showed in part how incompetent the federal side had been. Slightly more surprisingly, though not much, the report disclosed that the British Government had supplied more arms to the federal forces than it had disclosed. Total truthfulness has never seen much service as a weapon of war. More than two months later, in a move which senior ministers could have prevented had they wished, the police wheeled out section 2 of the Official Secrets Act 1911 as a means to prosecuting an oddly selective list of defendants: the editor of the *Sunday Telegraph* (Brian Roberts), the young journalist who got the story (Jonathan Aitken, later a Conservative MP), and a link in the chain by which he got it (Colonel Douglas Cairns) – but not the paper's editor-in-chief (Lord Hartwell), nor a former Conservative minister who also used the material (Hugh Fraser), nor a link man of higher rank (General Henry Alexander).

Section 2, hastily and widely drafted during a spy scare in the hot summer of 1911, made a blanket offence out of the unauthorized giving or receiving of any official information. When the case came on at the Old Bailey, a year after the event, the prosecution failed; and the judge (Mr Justice Caulfield) said in his summing-up:

> This case, if it does nothing more, may well alert those who govern us at least to consider, if they have time, whether or not section 2 of this Act has reached retirement age and should be pensioned off.

A committee was indeed set up under Lord Franks (yet another Oxford college head) to consider that question, and the committee did conclude – without immediate result – that section 2 should be repealed.

It was the Conservative Government under Edward Heath which set up Franks, since by the time the case came to trial the June 1970 election had intervened. Neither main party found its sympathy with the press increased by that election. It marked the high point of newspaper faith in opinion polls as guides to the way people would vote. Of lead stories in the national daily and Sunday press during the campaign, thirty out of ninety-six were about opinion polls. All the polls predicted a Labour win almost all the time. When the Conservatives won, senior politicians on both sides felt that the press had betrayed them: Labour, because Harold Wilson had been encouraged to run a self-destructively smug campaign; Conservative, because Edward Heath's lone gallantry in face of what everyone else believed certain defeat left him, after victory, an auto-crat among his colleagues.

All this time, broadcasting did not escape. It never could. During that same election, Labour charges of right-wing bias at the BBC were dismissed by Conservatives as merely an attempt to dissemble the BBC's left-wing bias. Politicians' developing animus against the media was particularly virulent against television, on the old ground of its near-magic power; and in the affairs of broadcasting it was the State – the apparatus which politicians controlled or aspired to control – which held the ultimate weapon as licenser. Journalists working in television became uneasily aware that the medium was in danger of becoming an arm of Government.

They had been reminded of their precarious standing by the ITV franchise reshuffle of June 1967: one Sunday morning Lord Hill, the ITA chairman, announced that in the next round of contracts two of the fifteen programme companies which made up the ITV network were to be merged, one was to have its territory halved and one was to have its licence taken away altogether. The decisions seemed based in great part on caprice, and had very little effect towards the desired aim of increasing the regionality of the companies and the variety of their output. One of the resulting new companies, London Weekend, won its contract by making promises which it was flagrantly unable to redeem. But Lord Hill was the Government-appointed head of a Government-established body, and his action was a reminder of where power lay.

The point was driven home six weeks later when Hill – as much to his own surprise as anyone else's – was appointed to the corresponding eminence (the chairmanship of the governors) at the BBC. Harold Wilson, as Prime Minister, was able to set over the BBC the representative of an organization which stood for different aims in broadcasting and had done the BBC great harm. Hill's replacement at the ITA was Lord Aylestone, a man with no other perceptible qualifications for the post than that he too had been a Cabinet minister. ITV already had a record of discreet sensitivity to politicians' wishes. At the BBC the signs of change were that Sir Hugh Greene ceased to be Director-General, and Mrs Whitehouse's protests were treated with a new respect.

In the recriminatory atmosphere which followed the 1970 election, with a Labour Opposition robbed of its expectations and a Conservative Government once again discovering the difficulty of redeeming its election pledges (about fewer civil servants, less subsidy to industry, and so on), complaints against the broadcasters flew. They were helped along by a streak of callow contempt which many broadcast interviewers took on as easily as they picked up certain broadcasting intonations. In June 1971 a BBC television programme called *Yesterday's Men* gave great offence for pouring genial scorn on Labour's fallen leaders and the way they now made their living. (Much of the trouble was that Labour politicians who helped make the film were not told what the title would be – though there was a certain rough justice about it, since the phrase had been first devised by Labour as an election cry against Conservative leaders.)

The row gave new impetus to Hill's search for a changed system of hearing complaints against the BBC; and in October 1971 a trio of eminent retired public servants was unveiled for the purpose. The ITA established a comparable body. But far from heading off criticism, the changes encouraged it. They were read as a sign that the BBC's governors, and the ITA, had lost the power to watch the public interest themselves. Among MPs there was renewed pressure for overt parliamentary control of broadcasting. Broadcast journalism risked losing some of the liberties which newspapermen had won for it.

During the same period, the BBC had to turn its mind to a medium it had all but forgotten: radio. Since the late 1950s, after the coming of ITV, the general preoccupation in broadcasting had been with television. Able young men and women in the BBC wanted to work in television, not radio. There was a widespread expectation, in that era of limitless technological self-confidence, that everything radio could do would be somehow taken over by its more advanced derivative. Radio would simply fade away. But it refused to. Obstinately, people went on buying radio sets: in 1964 they bought four million, as against one and a half million televison sets. Radio was saved by the discovery of its huge advantage over television: you could do something else while you listened. You could cook a meal, paint a room, drive a car; whereas the only activity which went at all easily with watching television was eating, and even then the intermittent need to look at your plate or cut a piece of bread or fetch another course ensured exactly that inattentiveness in the audience which was one of television's chief limitations.

Even so, the BBC might have kept its radio services going in a bored and mechanical spirit if it had not been for the pirate radio stations. During the early 1960s a number of enterprising groups, basing themselves on this continuing popularity of radio, discovered that if they broadcast into the United Kingdom from outside its territorial limits they could escape the rules to which the BBC owed its monopoly, reach a large British audience, collect a handsome advertising revenue, and pay none of it away in royalties on the recorded popular music which was their sole offering. As long as they were more than three miles offshore, the arm of the law could not touch them. Disused forts in the Thames estuary, ships anchored off Essex and the Isle of Man, even circling aircraft were all used for the purpose. The pirates had a short life: in January 1965 a number of north European countries similarly affected agreed to take common action, and at Westminster this issued in the Marine Broadcasting (Offences) Act 1967. It starved the broadcasters out by making it an offence, among other things, to supply them with advertising; and with continental refuges closed to them, they slowly died away. But they had reminded the BBC that there existed great numbers of listeners whose interests it was not meeting.

That by itself, again, might not have been enough. The BBC had long ago decided that there were tastes which, even as a national broadcaster, it was not in business to indulge, and a taste for unremitting popular music was one of them. But the pirates also reminded the Conservative party of its commitment to commercial broadcasting. For ten years after the authorizing of commercial television (during all of which time the Conservatives were in power) there had been no political interest in commercial radio. Compared with television, it looked absurdly unprofitable. But in the Conservative manifesto for the 1964 and 1966 elections, brief and cloudy phrases about choice in broadcasting reappeared. The BBC thereupon set its anxiety to preserve its radio monopoly above its anxiety to protect the national taste in music, and decided to strike first.

In September 1967 the BBC's three radio networks were redistributed into four, and renamed. The old Light, Third and Home programmes became in effect Radios 2, 3 and 4; and resources were found for a new channel, Radio 1, which broadcast very little but popular music (pausing every now and again to announce in song that 'Radio One is Wonderful'). In November the BBC began an experiment in local radio, in Leicester. Astute Conservatives had realized that the way to sell commercial broadcasting this second time was not as an escape from State monopoly but as a community service. The BBC was seeking to make the establishment of commercial radio needless by stepping in first with the two chief elements which commercial radio could thus be expected to provide: a great deal of pop music, and some kind of local flavour. In July 1969 a BBC document called *Broadcasting in the Seventies* announced a further stage in the policy of dividing the radio networks according to function, and therefore abandoning the old aim of periodically confronting the listener with something a little more demanding than he had expected; and in the autumn of 1970, eight further BBC local radio stations were opened.

The ploy did not work. It hardly deserved to, since it had been a renunciation of ends (certain notions of good broadcasting) in favour of means (preserving the tattered remnant of the BBC's monopoly). In March 1971 the Heath Government, in power only since June 1970, put out a White Paper which presented the case for commercial radio (cmnd 4636, par. 17):

> Now that radio presents current affairs in greater depth and often in a more controversial style, it is all the more important to offer the listener the choice of an alternative source of national and international radio news. Local advertising on radio will provide a new and useful service to the consumer, particularly the housewife. At the local level, the independent stations will have the opportunity to combine wide appeal with a first class service of local news and local information.

In June 1972 the Sound Broadcasting Act became law. In October 1973 the first commercial stations went on the air. Some of the contractors were unluckily chosen: the Independent Broadcasting Authority (as the ITA was now renamed) made a virtue of inexperience, notably in the contractors chosen for the London station which was to provide the 'alternative source of national and international radio news'. Much of the programming was infinitely banal. In cities where the BBC and the commercial interest met, they naturally competed by copying one another: choice was an illusion. Given the recession, there was not even the comfort that fortunes were being made. But the process was irreversible. By November 1973 the BBC had twenty local stations on the air. Within three years of that date the commercial total was up to nineteen.

Once arrived, the new competitor had at least one good effect on the BBC. For years, BBC radio had been cool to the kind of programme where listeners talked direct to the studio by telephone and were broadcast doing it. These phone-in programmes, borrowed from the United States, were a staple of commercial broadcasting from the first. During the two 1974 general elections, phone-ins to leading politicians on BBC radio every morning were the first innovation in British electioneering for years, and produced a mass of intelligent discussion.

In that way, and because of the narrow focus of local news, the change went a little way towards meeting the demand then current that the media should be accessible to others besides journalists and public figures. It was a demand that could never be met on any significant scale, given the limitations in time and space within which the media must work; but radio was best placed to make a gesture in that direction, needing less cumbrous equipment than television and offering fewer chances for editorial interference than newspapers.

The Open University was a related development. Starting in January 1971 at the instigation of the second Wilson Government, its dons taught the student body over the air and then marked the written work sent back to them by post. It was an exercise in 'access' broadcasting, to the extent that people who were not professional broadcasters were given a block of air time and allowed to fill it as they liked; and the bulk of it was carried on radio. In the 1970s it was the only kind of development which came easily. Neither the personal nor the corporate wealth was there for the expansion in television which had once seemed imminent – programmes round the clock, specialized news transmissions to subscribers, home videotape. Radio benefited.

So did newspapers. The recession which held their advertising revenue down did at least ensure that they were not also losing readers and revenue to electronic innovations. But they had other things to trouble them. Many of the recurrent issues which divide media and Government were exemplified in a series of peculiarly bitter rows in the early 1970s; and the newspapers bore the heat of the struggle.

The first such quarrel was about the degree of exposure which dissent from received social or moral attitudes properly deserved. Noticeable dissenters were the periodicals which made up the underground press. They were not underground papers in the French Resistance sense of being passed from hand to hand surreptitiously and in fear: in London and many university towns they could be bought at bookstalls. The metaphor was the one used in the title of the early-nineteenth-century radical paper *Black Dwarf*: it suggested a tiny pioneer undermining the known social landscape. These newspapers addressed a variety of special groups, but they had common antipathies. They were against industrialization, war, and restraints of any kind on behaviour, particularly when applied by agents of the State. They believed, in face of all the evidence the other way, in the natural goodness of man.

The earliest such journal to appear in the United Kingdom was the *International Times*, or *IT*. It published its first number in London in October 1966, under the distant impulse of the student revolution which had begun not long before in California. It was soon joined by others. (*Private Eye*, which dated from five years earlier, could not be classified with this group. Its editors did not dissent from the established order: they simply noticed that it was often absurdly and sometimes dishonestly run.) The problem for the organizers of the underground press was that they had to pay their printers like anybody else; and to make money from sales and advertisements they had to concentrate on the likeliest interests of the young readers they aimed at – pop music, drugs of certain kinds, uninhibited sex.

This bent kept them from being understood by the middle-aged, middle-class, middle-opinion people whom they most needed to address if their protests were to have effect; and it gave rise to a body of indignation which came to a head in May 1971 when one of them, *Oz*, in a vein of desperate and unsuccessful overstatement, published a 'schoolkids' issue' which contained matter ostensibly written by and for children about unconventional sexual practices. At the instigation of the Director of Public Prosecutions the paper's three editors were charged, under the Obscene Publications Act 1959, with offences which ordinarily carried fines. In August, after a long and disorderly jury trial at the Old Bailey, the three were sentenced to prison terms of between nine and fifteen months instead.

It was in an odd way the underground press's moment in the sun. Even Conservative newspapers protested against the sentences; they were quashed on appeal; and sales of *Oz* went up, briefly. The attempt at censorship on moral grounds had met with its ordinary penalty of ridicule. Yet the Old Bailey jury, as juries should, had accurately reflected a general judgement. Underground newspapers had reached their limit of public notice and approval, and thereafter declined from it. *Oz* closed in May 1973. It was a pity: the resulting gap was in part filled by totally un-idealistic pornographers.

There followed a succession of disputes where the newspaper principally engaged happened to be the *Sunday Times*. In August 1971 the British Army, having tried for two years unavailingly to pacify Northern Ireland, was persuaded to intern some hundreds of suspected republican insurgents – to imprison them without term or trial. In

October 1971 the *Sunday Times* published evidence that a handful of these people, once interned, had been interrogated by methods which threatened their sanity; and in November the paper carried two long pieces reviewing British involvement in Northern Ireland and tracing the resurgence of the Irish Republican Army largely to British heavy-handedness. It was a dispute which has arisen in every war. Ministers believed that the newspaper was giving moral support to an enemy of the State; the newspaper felt that the citizens of that State deserved to know what methods were being used in preserving it. The conflict of duties lessened as the reproach of ineptitude and cruelty shifted more and more from the British to the republican side; but tension was bound to persist in some form as long as the Northern Ireland emergency itself did.

Disputes between journalists and politicians could also arise out of brushes with the law. There is in most respects a separation between the politicians who make the law and the lawyers who decide what it means. But the Lord Chancellor, the head of the judiciary, sits in the Cabinet; and the Attorney-General, the Government's senior legal adviser, is an MP and a minister. When these men find themselves ranged against a newspaper, the Government is embroiled. The drug thalidomide provided a case in point. Between 1959 and 1962 some 8000 children were born deformed in different parts of the world because their mothers, at a certain stage of pregnancy, had taken thalidomide (under a variety of names) as a tranquillizer or a sleeping pill. In the United Kingdom, where there were some 400 such cases, the issue of compensation took more than a decade to settle in the courts; and during that time many of the families had poverty as well as misery to contend with. The drug had been developed in Germany, and marketed in Britain by a subsidiary of the huge liquor firm Distillers. Distillers denied negligence, and for ten years were able to hold off any significant press comment on the compensation claims by making clear that the company would seek to have it proceeded against as contempt of court.

In December 1971 the *Daily Mail* made one sortie across this shadowy frontier without ill consequence; and in September 1972 the *Sunday Times* published a leading article which said that the whole story shamed our society and the law and Distillers, and that Distillers 'should offer much, much more' than they were then offering. The leader was supported with a long article about the unsound basis on which such claims were assessed, and in later weeks with case histories well designed to move public sympathy.

The outcome was inconclusive. On the immediately important point, Distillers did generously increase their compensation offer the following year from £3·25 million to some £20 million. The claims were ultimately settled on that figure, and a Royal Commission was set up under Lord Pearson on the law relating to personal injuries. But although the Attorney-General, who settles whether there should be contempt-of-court proceedings, decided not to move against the *Sunday Times* over the original leader and article, he did initiate an action which kept the paper from publishing a further article explaining how thalidomide had come to be marketed at all. (That injunction, upheld by the House of Lords as the highest court of appeal, was not lifted till June 1976; the article, six pages in length, was published the next Sunday.) Moreover, there was no universal agreement that the processes of the law were faulty. Before Distillers improved their offer there had been public talk of boycotting their products, and institutional shareholders had become seriously worried. A good many lawyers, and some politicians, felt that the *Sunday Times* had distorted the judicial process. The *Law Society's Gazette* wrote in January 1973: 'The campaign had all the subtlety and legal justification of Robin Hood's activities in Sherwood Forest.'

In the month after the original *Sunday Times* excursus about thalidomide, another report in the same paper re-opened the argument about Government secrets. The article disclosed, on the basis of documents examined, that the Department of the Environment was thinking of reducing British Rail's losses by tearing up half its track. It was by no stretch of the imagination a secret touching the security of the State. Yet the police – briefed by the Director of Public Prosecutions, who had been briefed by the Department – cautioned the editor of the *Sunday Times* under the Official Secrets Act, and raided the offices of the *Railway Gazette* (a magazine suspected of complicity) on a warrant issued under the Theft Act, before it was decided that there was not enough evidence for prosecutions. Edward Heath and others of his ministers were indignant that one option among many should be published before the Government had decided it was to be adopted. The newspaper maintained that it was exactly then, while the decision could still be affected, that there ought to be public discussion. The railway track survived.

The last of this group of disputes was the affair of the Crossman diaries. Richard Crossman died early in April 1974. He had been an Oxford tutor in political philosophy as a young man, and later a Cabinet minister in the first and second Wilson Governments, and he had then kept diaries whose chief interest he believed to be that they would 'provide a unique historical record of how British Cabinet Government operated in the 1960s'. They contained accounts, strikingly though not unprecedentedly explicit, of positions taken by ministers and officials in high-level policy arguments. Before the end of the month in which Crossman died the *Sunday Times* announced, by arrangement with his literary executors, that it would publish serial extracts from the diaries in the autumn. Sir John Hunt, the Cabinet Secretary, acting with the approval of Harold Wilson, who was then back in office as Prime Minister, sought to exercise a right of custom and stop them. His case was that there could never otherwise be uninhibited discussion in the seats of power again. But the newspaper made just enough concessions by omission to be able to begin publication in January 1975 without incurring action under the Official Secrets Act, and then advanced week by week in boldness gradually enough to keep the same immunity. The Government did then make an attempt in the courts to prevent publication of the diaries in book form, mainly as a breach of confidence. The effort failed; but the Lord Chief Justice's judgement was unspecific enough on certain points to make sure that the basic dispute – which was about whether the confidentiality of Cabinet discussion was either necessary to good government or secured by law – would continue.

The case for the diaries was not entirely high-souled. Material showing public men and women to be no more than human, as several passages did, may be absorbing without being important. Conservative ministers had already been reminded of that in June 1973, when two of their number (Lord Lambton and Lord Jellicoe) had been obliged to resign when they were discovered to have consorted with prostitutes. Not merely had the disclosures been made in part by the *News of the World* and the *Sunday People* through the use of surreptitious bedroom photography, but they were unimportant in themselves. They had no interest beyond salacity. Politicians on both sides of the House saw it as evidence of incurable frivolity, and were only confirmed in that view by the general glee at Crossman's incidental malice.

There were other quarrels. The fourth and last Wilson administration, from March 1974 to April 1976, infuriated newspaper editors by its insistence on re-legalizing closed shops without exempting newspapers. (The issue is examined in chapter 6 of this book.) Relations between Wilson's Press Secretary and the corps of political correspondents known as the Lobby worsened to the point where in June 1975 their organized daily encounters were broken off, though a vast apparatus for putting out Government and party information remained. The issue of Cabinet secrecy was revived in June 1976, after James Callaghan had come to power, when the weekly *New Society* accurately narrated a Cabinet dispute which had ended in a retreat from a new system of child benefit. In the same month the fall of Jeremy Thorpe from the Liberal leadership left a quantity of bad blood. He was charged by an old acquaintance, from within the protected setting of a magistrates' court, with having once been a homosexual; and the press, unable (since the law did not) to treat homosexuality as an offence and yet egged on from within the Liberal party, picked at the ill-judged reticence of Thorpe and his friends for four months until the reticence itself seemed culpable and Thorpe had to resign.

One reason why politicians found this prurience troubling was that there was talk at the time of State economic help for newspapers. Harold Wilson had spoken in February 1976 of 'supposedly bankrupt newspapers, holding out their hands for public money, wasting money in what is a classic innuendo against an MP' – which illustrated why newspapers were in fact reluctant to take public money, since the clearly expected quid pro quo would be an unquestioning respect for public men. The times were certainly bad for newspapers: because advertising is always one of the first things to be reduced in a recession, newspapers are among the first sufferers. Wilson's fourth Government had itself brought the notion of a State-funded press a little nearer. A new Glasgow daily, the *Scottish Daily News*, had been given six months of struggling life as a workers' co-operative because Tony Benn, as Industry Secretary, lent it nearly half its working capital. The experiment lasted from May to November 1975 before the dearth of readers destroyed it. More than that, a Royal Commission on the Press which had been routinely established in July 1974 was asked by the Department of Trade in September 1975 'to examine urgently the financial situations and immediate prospects of the national newspapers'. The impetus, it was true, had come from the Newspaper Publishers' Association as well as the General Secretaries of the newspaper unions; but the hope was of waking the whole industry to the realities more than of persuading ministers to pay its losses. In an interim report published (cmnd 6433) in March 1976, the Commission nevertheless proposed that the State should give newspapers interest-relief on the loans they would need if they were to modernize their printing methods and cut their costs. Although no action followed for the time being, the idea was not ruled out.

This Royal Commission, under Professor O. R. McGregor, a London University social historian, took its place in the third pair of media inquiries since the Second World War. It arose out of the same accumulated governmental irritation with the press as the first two press commissions, and found itself addressing much the same problems: who should control newspapers, whether their range of political sympathies might be broadened, how they should behave. The parallel inquiry was a Committee on Broadcasting under Lord Annan, Provost of University College London. The Annan Committee's main task was to decide what should happen to the industry once the BBC's and the ITV companies' right to broadcast (which had been extended by three years) lapsed at the end of July 1979; and the Committee had also to take account of technical change, which offered an extra television channel besides the two used by the BBC and the one by ITV. Lord Annan had been first appointed by the second Wilson Government just before the June 1970 election. He was stood down by the incoming Heath Government, which pardonably believed that equally sound advice to ministers could be assembled with less fuss by civil servants; but he was reappointed in April 1974 when Labour came back to power.

One long-running argument, at any rate, was half settled. After a few timid closed-circuit adventures in both Houses of Parliament, parts of the proceedings of the Commons were broadcast on radio for four weeks in June and July 1975. The experiment was a clear success: whatever television might do, radio could 'put the people more closely in touch with Parliament' (in the words of a Commons Select Committee report, *The Experiment in Public Sound Broadcasting*, January 1976, par. 1) without altering it in the process; and in March 1976 both Commons and Lords decided to make the broadcasts permanent from the following session – though the Commons then took so long to approve the details that there was no possibility of any actual transmissions before 1978.

PART TWO

Institutions and groups

Chapter 4: Owners

So the struggle, when the media have come into the post-war political argument, has been an increasingly sharp one between people anxious to exert a measure of control over the press or broadcasting and people actually exerting it. The would-be controllers are easy enough to spot: they are for the most part politicians, legitimately representing Governments or parties or interest groups or themselves. Identifying the actual controllers is more difficult. Influence is dispersed. It is distributed among several groups and institutions, all worth examining. The most prominent such group is the body of people who have the media in their ownership.

In broadcasting, this group excites little passion. The BBC is legally a body corporate whose members are its twelve governors. They are appointed for fixed terms by the State, and the State does part of their work by making conditions about how the BBC must conduct itself.

Commercial broadcasting companies are privately owned; but the owners are contracted to continue broadcasting for a fixed term of years, again on the State's conditions, and they may have to forfeit their franchise at the end of it and submit to a forced sale of their assets. Profits are permissible, and big profits have sometimes been made; but ownership is dispersed under rules made from time to time by the IBA, the State's regulatory agency. In 1964 the Thomson Organization owned 80 per cent of the voting shares in Scottish Television. The IBA had the holding reduced to 55 per cent, and four years later to 25 per cent. The influence of individual shareholders is fragmented and haphazard. Ownership is no more a dominant force in commercial broadcasting than it is at the BBC. If it mattered, programmes from the two sources would differ more than they do.

It is the ownership of newspapers which is contentious. With insignificant exceptions like staff newspapers in Government departments, they are all in private hands. Historically it has seemed an obvious development. When newspapers were first thought of, early in the seventeenth century, they were seen as an enemy of Government rather than an adjunct; and the idea of State participation in mere commercial enterprise was a great way off. So the money for printing presses had to come from private capital if it was to come from anywhere. By the time advances in literacy and printing technology had made mass-circulation newspapers possible, in the latter part of the nineteenth century, successive Governments had been forced to give up the licensing and taxation controls they had. Nothing fettered private ownership except the ordinary law.

The first modern newspaper proprietor on those terms was Alfred Harmsworth, who founded the *Daily Mail* in 1896 and became Lord Northcliffe in 1905. The popular picture of the newspaper baron is still largely drawn from Northcliffe: capricious and autocratic. Whether his current anxiety was that the Navy should build battleships or Britons should eat wholemeal bread, he was able to make sure that *Mail* readers learnt of it day after day. He deluged his staff with written instructions and comments. He was known to avoid Ludgate Circus, the main crossroads of the London newspaper district, in case he met any of the multitudinous journalists he had sacked. He reminded his own staff of the emperor Nero.

His younger brother Harold, who became Lord Rothermere and took on the *Mail* after Northcliffe's death in 1922, changed enthusiasms and editors with gloomy abandon. Max Aitken, Lord Beaverbrook, who bought a controlling interest in the *Daily Express* in 1916 and hugely increased its circulation, used it to pursue his dream of making the British empire an economic unity long after the imperial idea had ceased to be a political reality, and bullied his editors by telephone to make sure they did not backslide. There were others, all peers. A family of newspaper-men from South Wales called Berry acquired as many newspaper directorships, and titles, as the Harmsworths themselves. These men could comment on what they liked, and themselves escape comment. Other men's illegitimate children or symptoms of insanity might be held matters of public interest; not Northcliffe's.

Yet by the time Beaverbrook died in June 1964, at the age of 85, the breed was dead. He and Northcliffe had had no successors of comparable talent, and once the inventors of the style were gone its imitators began to look merely absurd. From the early 1960s there was a general revolt against the notion of power exercised by right of wealth or inherited position; Harold Wilson made good use of the sentiment in winning the October 1964 election; and journalists, perceiving the change in the course of their work, began to bring it into their own affairs. In January 1964 Roy Thomson, who more than four years before had bought out a Berry (Lord Kemsley) as owner of the *Sunday Times*, did become one of the last hereditary peers created; but even while he waited for the honour, the *Sunday Times* cheerfully attacked the Prime Minister, Sir Alec Douglas-Home, through whom ennoblement would come if it came at all.

Proprietors disappeared from editorial conferences. The decision about what news to cover, and what to say about it in leaders, was left to staff journalists. *The Times* already had a long tradition of immunity from proprietorial whims. That had been established after an unhappy fourteen years during which Northcliffe himself owned the paper before his death; and the tradition was not disturbed when Thomson bought control from the Astor family at the end of 1966. By the 1970s Lord Beaverbrook's son, and the first Lord Rothermere's grandson, kept their minds at the *Express* and the *Mail* on money rather than policy.

They had little alternative, because they had few sanctions. Editors had grown cunning: when they took office they saw to it that they became expensive to dismiss. They were themselves not autocrats. Their own staffs felt a new security, because of new laws against unfair dismissal and the increasing strength of the National Union of Journalists. So they too were prepared to risk the displeasure of superiors by asking for a share in their paper's decisions. At each level, dictatorship had to give way to discussion. By the mid-1970s the last remaining instance of a principal shareholder who acted as editor-in-chief on his own newspapers was another Berry, Lord Hartwell, at the *Daily Telegraph* and the *Sunday Telegraph*. But his editors told him their leader topics after the leaders were written, not before.

The *Guardian* has been owned since 1936, and the *Observer* was owned between 1945 and 1976, by a trust. What marks a trust off from other forms of ownership is not that it makes no profits. That has been a common enough condition, even among newspaper managements which have taken profit as an aim. The difference in a trust is that the trustees themselves are of equal weight with one another, and change regularly. None, therefore, is in a position to build up personal power, and the newspaper's staff is left to get on with the job. Something of the same result follows when newspapers belong to big commercial groups with varied interests (like the American oil company to which the *Observer* passed), where the top men have global problems of trade and investment to occupy their minds.

Yet these are capitalist organizations. So are trusts. However tamed, the heirs to Northcliffe and Beaverbrook are still private owners. The private holding and venturing of capital is a practice prized by the Conservative party in particular. The possibility remains that newspapers so owned will have an inclination towards Conservative ways of thought, whether they mean to or not. The time may have gone by when – as happened to the *Pall Mall Gazette*, a London evening paper, in 1893 – a Liberal newspaper could be sold to a Conservative politician (W. W. Astor, an

immigrant American) and become a Conservative paper
overnight, while the editor was on holiday. (He and his
deputy – the young J. A. Spender, later a well-known
Liberal editor himself – left the paper.) It may be true that
there are now no national newspapers which depend on
Conservative party subsidy, as the *Globe* (another London
evening paper) and even the *Observer* did before the First
World War; nor, for that matter, are there any which owe
their continued existence to Liberal financial patronage,
like the *Daily News* (for which in 1900 Lloyd George found
Liberal buyers led by George Cadbury) or the *Daily
Chronicle* (which for eight years after the war he owned
himself). Nevertheless, the newspaper industry remains
almost exclusively in private hands; and for as long as the
tussle between private and public ownership is taken to be
one of the central disputes in politics, and the private side
is espoused mainly by the Conservatives, then there is a
case for supposing that the press must be predominantly
Conservative in its sympathies.

That was certainly part of the argument which in 1912
impelled George Lansbury, the Labour leader, to revive a
small strike sheet called the *Daily Herald* as a regular
morning paper. But its initial capital, laboriously subscribed
on appeal, was only £300; doses of union money after the
war could not protect it against loss; a 51 per cent share was
ceded to commercial publishers, Odhams, in 1929; and the
Herald collapsed for lack of readers in 1964. Its ultimate
heir, the tabloid *Sun*, became largely non-political. Although
the *Scottish Daily News* was a workers' co-operative, it
was founded chiefly as a protest at the way 1800 Beaverbrook employees lost their jobs in Glasgow when production
of the *Scottish Daily Express* and the *Scottish Sunday
Express* was shifted to Manchester and the Glasgow *Evening
Citizen* closed; and in its six-month life during 1975 the
new paper had no chance to develop policies appropriate to
its constitution or even machinery to evolve them. Among
daily papers only the Communist *Morning Star*, founded

in 1930 as the *Daily Worker* and never widely read, was left as a declared anti-capitalist voice.

It can be argued on the other side that capitalist-owned newspapers have not always taken capitalist positions. Although many people on the left wing in politics persisted into the 1970s in regarding the tug between public and private ownership of resources as the key divide, there were voices in the Labour party which claimed as early as the 1950s that the issue had lost its importance. Newspapers, certainly, did not behave as if it was the one question which must be allowed to determine all others. They were never inhibited from criticizing the party of private ownership and supporting its Labour opponents. In most general elections since the Second World War, support for the two main parties has been about equal, in the sense that roughly the same number of papers has been sold on either side of the argument. Even if that had not been so, and the weight of electoral support had been for the Conservatives, they would have enjoyed no necessary advantage. The two general elections of 1974 were not the only ones in which the voters disregarded a preponderance of pro-Conservative newspaper advice. The Liberals won in a landslide in 1906 in spite of having nearly all the big circulations against them.

That is perhaps to take the question of newspaper political influence too literally. There are other forms of conservatism besides advocating a Conservative vote at general elections. A claim often made is that in the referendum held in June 1975 about whether the United Kingdom should stay in the European Economic Community, the heavy press support for a 'yes' vote – which proved to be the winning side – was a kind of conservatism, because most of the Conservative party and most of the business community were of that mind. But so were the Liberals and a fair slice of the Labour party; there were idealistic as well as materialistic arguments on both sides; and it is at least possible that the newspapers were predominantly on that side because it was on balance the right one.

The case is more easily sustained as the issues covered in newspapers become less openly political. It may well be that newspapers are disposed to uphold the ordering of society much as they find it. That kind of conservatism would go well beyond the choice of which political speech to report, or which party's policy to back in the leader columns. It would colour the coverage of religion, and social ideas, and sport, and the arts, and fashion. Even at that the case is not clear: the mark from which conservatism is measured is a shifting one, fixed only in the mind of the reader, and a great deal less identifiable than the divide between political parties. There is not a cohesive corpus of radical ideas whose recurrence in several newspapers would refute the general charge. Most people's radicalism is patchy: political revolutionaries (like the Provisionals in Northern Ireland) are often fiercely conservative over matters of faith and family morality. Still, if a suitable calculus could be arrived at, it could probably be used to show journalists tending in general to assume that the way life is at present organized is the right way – that it may need improvement, but not overthrow.

If that tendency did exist, it would be no surprise. Newspapers demand heavy and recurrent capital investment: the McGregor Commission's interim report suggested £20 million as the sum which the national newspapers would need to spend during the final four years of the 1970s in going over from hot-metal printing to cold-type photo-setting. Organizations which invested that kind of money could not help preferring a world where the rights of property were respected and the future reliably predictable from the past. Newspapers are produced and distributed at speed by a succession of complicated processes, and they miss their moment if they are more than a few hours late: they have special reason for wanting a society where strikes are few and the trains run on time.

More than all that, newspapers depend on literacy. It has been said of tabloid newspapers that they are 'written by people who can't write for people who can't read'; but the phrase is telling just because it shows how such papers can deny their proper nature. All newspapers demand a measure of literacy in their readers. Popular papers keep the demand as gentle as they can: they deal in short words, short sentences, few paragraphs of more than a single sentence, few articles of more than a few paragraphs, and a great many pictures. But the readers still have to know their letters, and to be able to exclude the rest of the world for long enough to use the skill. From their writers, newspapers expect a high degree of literacy (though they do not always get it). Anyone who writes for newspapers for a living is likely to have come to it from an earlier interest in writing, which will itself have been nourished by an interest in reading; and there will be a great deal of reading still to be done, even if it is only of other newspapers, Government documents and public-relations handouts. It is possible to read in bus queues and newspaper newsrooms; learned minds have been furnished wholly out of public libraries; but profitable reading ordinarily presupposes that the reader possesses a number of books, has had a background and education which furthers understanding of them, and can read them in the kind of comfort and silence which go with middle-class affluence and attitudes.

Clearly there have been radicals, tending all the way to anarchists, who have been highly literate. The glory of the written word is that there is no idea which it cannot compass. But it is probably true that people who write in newspapers are, by virtue of the very experiences which have prepared them for their work, inclined to exalt a stable above a revolutionary world.

Next there are the consequences which follow from newspapers being not merely capitalist but also commercial organizations. By the end of 1976 only the *Guardian* and the *Telegraph* papers, among national newspapers, were private concerns. The rest belonged to large public companies; and many of those were groups with diverse trading interests far beyond newspapers – Associated Newspapers (which owned the *Daily Mail*), Pearson Longman (the *Financial Times*), Reed International (*Daily Mirror*, *Sunday Mirror*, *Sunday People*), the Thomson Organization (*The Times* and the *Sunday Times*), Atlantic Richfield (the *Observer*). Given the great cost of sustaining a modern newspaper, that seemed likely to be the spreading pattern of future ownership.

Such an arrangement imposes its own restraints, certainly. In the nature of things, the *Financial Times* cannot report on Pearson Longman's interests in book-publishing as unselfconsciously as it would on the affairs of any other publisher; and neither the *Sunday Times* nor the *Observer* can write with absolute dispassion about the oil industry, where the Thomson Organization as well as Atlantic Richfield has large interests. More important, such commercial groups are ostensibly run solely to make a good living for the people who work or invest in them. If a newspaper is not contributing its share to a group's profits, it might in theory find itself instructed by the group's men of business to change its ways so that it could contribute. If it persisted in making a loss, its commercial management might think right to pay off the paper's workers and amputate the offending member. It has happened. The most notable case, which still echoes in the folk memory of Fleet Street, was the closure in 1960 of the ailing *News Chronicle* by the Cadbury family, whose surviving interests spanned chocolate and television.

But there are things to be said on the other side. The difficulty over writing about a group's other interests is not a grave one. It is at any rate seldom tackled by publishing unfairly flattering accounts of them. Journalists are well aware that they will be believed only with difficulty if they praise their own employers, and never believed again if their praise turns out to be undeserved. In consequence their observations tend to be brief, and sometimes even unfairly cool. When a former editor of the *Economist*, Lord Crowther, went off into the boardroom world while keeping a connection with the paper, it was found wise to have a house rule that his business interests should not be written about at all. The men running Thomson's non-newspaper interests have concluded that being linked to a number of newspapers is 'a mild public-relations disadvantage'. But the disadvantage is not much felt by readers. If they want a clear-eyed account of the Thomson Organization's fortunes, there are plenty of other newspapers they can find it in. And a newspaper owned by a commercial group writes inhibitedly about a handful of concerns at most; a paper owned by the State, the effective alternative, would be guarded in its outlook on whole areas of the national life.

As for commercial interference, it is certainly true that newspapers have to live in the real world. It would be true under any system of ownership and finance. (Trust ownership did not cocoon the *Observer*.) Wage bills would still have to be met, ink and paper paid for; and the sums thus laid out could not over a period of time exceed the money coming in, whether it came from sales or advertisements or the Government or appeals at public meetings. Any commercial management would from time to time point that out, and would agree with the editorial management a figure for editorial spending which bore a measured relation to receipts. But once that budget was determined, there would be no need for the commercial managers to say anything else until the next year's budget meetings; and that is in fact how newspapers work. Editorial decisions are then taken on what are seen as their merits, not on commercial grounds at all.

The *News Chronicle* remains a salutary warning, and yet an oddly solitary one. National newspapers have been merged and closed since the Second World War; yet the *Chronicle* was the only victim which had real merit, and the total number of closures and mergers has been small compared with the total in other industries, some of which have been technically more innovative – the aircraft industry, for example, or the paint trade. More noticeable than closure has been the tendency of commercial managements to keep newspapers going when their commercial circumstances do not strictly warrant it. Here the most striking example has been *The Times*, which continued to lose about £1 million a year after Lord Thomson became its chief proprietor in January 1967, and which he and his family continued proudly to support. Businessmen and business organizations still seem to like owning newspapers: witness the number of tycoons, including Rupert Murdoch, who queued to lose money refinancing the *Observer*. The propaganda motive (which Beaverbrook maintained was his only purpose at the *Daily Express*) has been largely blocked by the developing independence of journalists and the check provided through broadcasting; but the spirit of public service never wholly dies, and sometimes there is also the meaner consideration that a national newspaper is difficult to close without attracting fiercely unfavourable notice.

Managements so placed prefer not to think of themselves as philanthropically saving a newspaper from extinction: they are tiding it over a bad period till it makes a profit again. There are undoubtedly cases where that is a true picture. The positive virtue in a newspaper's belonging to a larger commercial group is that the paper can take strength from the association. This can go beyond the merely financial. Where the group is wholly or in part a chain of newspapers, it can supply each newspaper with central help which the paper could not afford alone: reports from Westminster, for example, or from foreign capitals; expert advice in libel cases; encouragement to stand firm against local pressures. It was partly because the *Belfast Telegraph* had become a Thomson newspaper in 1961 that it was able to remain uniquely non-partisan during the strife which began seven years later.

There remains the question of the pursuit of readers. Even if everything else were explained away, many people's minds would still harbour the residual suspicion that commercial managements are in business to sell newspapers, and also to sell advertising space at a rate which is a function of the number of newspapers they sell, and that therefore their over-riding aim must always be to catch and keep as many readers as they can.

There are good grounds for the belief. It has hold of the central truth about newspapers: that they are what they are because human nature is what it is. The speed at which most of their contents are written, and judged, means that they reflect certain human reactions with an undissembled accuracy. Their content cannot exceed the capacity of their writers, clearly; but, even more limitingly, it cannot go beyond the range of their readers. It is therefore the readers, in the end, who are the figures of power.

But not any old readers. Each newspaper has its own group. *The Times*, the oldest daily paper still in publication, acknowledged this truth on the day it began (as the *Daily Universal Register*) in 1785:

> It would seem that every News-Paper published in London is calculated for a particular set of readers only; so that if each set were to change its favourite publication for another, the commutation would produce disgust, and dissatisfaction to all.

The paper declared that it was going to change all that, and offer 'something suited to every palate'. But the readers who choose a paper are not necessarily the readers whom the paper at first chooses. The newspaper cost the considerable sum of twopence-halfpenny, raised after three months to threepence; it carried mostly City news, with succinct political reports and a little information from abroad. The readers who took the paper up were from the mercantile class. Its founder, John Walter, was an able journalist, and *The Times* (as it became after three years) expanded its coverage; but it could only do so and stay solvent because the horizons of English merchants, at the time of the French Revolution and the ensuing war with France, were similarly expanding.

Northcliffe started the *Daily Mirror*, in November 1903, as 'a daily newspaper for gentlewomen'. Most of the editorial staff were gentlewomen too. Within three months the daily sale had fallen from 276,000 copies to 25,000. The gentlewomen were sacked, the *Mirror* became 'a paper for men and women', photographs (printed by a process developed under Northcliffe's patronage) were lavishly introduced, and the size and price were lowered. It was discovered that men and women, as distinct from gentlewomen, liked a cheap tabloid. A group of readers had made its choice.

Once a newspaper and its body of readers had come together, the readers remained the freer of the two. The paper could not attempt a fresh choice of reader without the risk of losing those it had; but any reader could choose a different paper. The paper could accustom its readers, over the years, to usages which they might not of themselves have welcomed; but it was itself modified by their attitudes, as expressed in their letters, their comments to members of the staff, the things they said in newsagents' shops as carried back by the paper's salesmen, and the rise or fall in sales which followed notable articles or pictures. Since journalists prefer if possible to work for papers they agree with and admire, the paper's readers came also to be more and more represented among its writers.

Between 1967 and 1970, under its new Thomson management, *The Times* made a serious attempt to extend its readers beyond the circle of what its own advertising termed 'top people'. Not enough of them were buying the paper: it was losing money heavily. But that very slogan, crude as it was – 'Top people take *The Times*' – had summed up the difficulty the paper was in. Its existing readers were people with firm and idiosyncratic views, nurtured over generations, about the way the news of the day should be approached and the language handled. Unless these notions were to a great extent disregarded, the charmed circle could not be significantly enlarged; yet if they were disregarded, the existing readers would be driven away, and the paper would be worse off than before. The effort was made still harder by the fact that with the November 1967 devaluation of sterling the years of postwar expansion in the economy came to an end. The attempt was abandoned in 1970.

The tastes of a body of readers may alter over the years. They change as the prevailing climate of ideas changes. They change as a result of what they discover to be appearing in rival newspapers. The *Daily Mirror* would never have begun (in the 1970s) to show photographs of naked women, or to lead the paper with stories like 'I married the monster who raped Miss X', if the *Sun* had not led the way after its change of ownership in 1969. Once the *Sun* had demonstrated that its readers liked that kind of approach, the *Mirror* adopted it too, and the decline in the *Mirror*'s circulation was at least checked. Yet it was not an expedient which was open to *The Times*, struggling for new readers at much the same time. Existing readers of *The Times* would have been outraged at being addressed in that way. The loss would have far outweighed the gain.

It is readers who determine the character of newspapers. The *Sun* illustrates the point in its simplest and saddest form. Until 1964 the *Daily Herald*, and between 1964 and 1969 the broadsheet *Sun*, had struggled to interest working people principally through their intellect. The paper had declined inexorably. Murdoch gave up the attempt and went for the baser instincts. Sales soared. It was an owner's decision, certainly; but it would have meant nothing without the enthusiastic ratification of the readers.

That, in the end, is the answer to the riddle of proprietorial influence. Where it survives at all, it must still defer to the influence of readers. The policy of the *Daily Telegraph*, its selection and opinion of the news it reports, is decided by the editor and his senior colleagues. But there is a regulatory force which keeps the paper's policy from straying too widely or suddenly from pre-ordained paths; and that force is not the proprietor but the readers. They chose the paper for qualities they expect to see continued.

The press is thus predominantly conservative in tone because its readers are. If any substantial number of people seriously wanted the structure of society rebuilt from the bottom, the *Morning Star* would sell more copies than it does. The reason why national newspapers fall tidily into two bundles – popular and posh, with the popular ones all physically smaller than the posh (since the *Daily Express* joined the other tabloids in January 1977) but selling five times as many copies – is that British life remains similarly and obstinately divided. The steady lessening of the economic differences between classes has done nothing to narrow the cultural gap. Certainly there are people who read both a posh and a popular paper, just as there are gradations between the popular papers: both the *Mirror* and the *Sun* aim at readers who are more squarely working-class than the *Express* and the *Mail* do. These things show the complexity of the class pattern, without denying its general lines. The broad shape and nature of the press is ultimately determined by no one but its readers.

Chapter 5: Advertisers

The second group of people and organizations who wield a measure of control over the media are advertisers. Advertisements have been a significant part of newspapers almost since newspapers began. If you wanted to buy or sell an article or a service, a newspaper could be a great help. It was likely to reach more people than a notice pinned to a wall, or the voice of a crier, ever could; and a newspaper was a more precise instrument, too, in that it was likely to be read only by the kind of people which its contents indicated. A publisher could advertise in a journal read by literary men; a man with cargo space to sell in his ship could choose a paper for merchants. Neither dissipated his effort.

This importance was recognized in titles. As early as 1730 there was a newspaper called the *Daily Advertiser*; and for more than two centuries after that it was common practice to put nothing but advertisements on the front page. Several local weekly papers preserve both usages to this day.

The attractiveness of newspaper advertising increased rapidly in the second half of the nineteenth century as circulations did. Improved printing methods, cheap paper and fast distribution by train came to meet an expanding lower middle class. Northcliffe's achievement, when he founded the *Daily Mail* at the end of the century, was to give these new newspaper-readers – and especially the women among them – better value for money than they had had before; and the trick was worked through advertising. It was the increased advertisement revenue made possible by a mass market which enabled him truthfully to claim, as he did in the top left-hand corner of the front page of the *Mail*'s very first issue, that he was selling 'a penny newspaper for one halfpenny'.

Northcliffe always had a split mind about advertisements. He complained constantly to his advertising staff about their prominence and ugliness. He was half aware that there might be a price to be paid for the new resources they brought to his newspapers. But he had hastened a development which he could not stop. Newspapers which sought to match the *Mail*'s coverage at the same price had to go after the same sources of revenue. Competition made the change permanent.

The money was well used. The cheapest way to run a newspaper is to have it all put together by staff journalists who never leave the building. The moment you send them out in search of information, or employ experts – China-watchers, tennis correspondents, gardening writers – whose services you will not need every day, your costs rise. The more comprehensive a newspaper is, and the more detailed and far-flung the expertise it draws on, the more expensive it is to run – and in the post-Northcliffe era the more depen-dent on advertising revenue. On all national newspapers, the proportion of income from advertising, as against sales to readers, rose steadily through the first half of the twentieth century; but by the time it had reached half at papers like the *Mail*, it was up to three-quarters at papers like *The Times*.

The ultimate development of the system would be a news-paper wholly financed by advertising, and given away to its readers for nothing. Such newspapers exist, but only on a limited and local scale. The whole operation has seemed too haphazard, both to advertisers and to newspaper publishers, for the attempt to have been made nationally. Nothing would ensure that distribution was conscientiously done, or that the sole source of funds kept a constant level. More than that, it is reasonable to doubt whether the public at large would wholly believe what it learnt from publica-tions whose main aim was not to inform or entertain it but to sell it things.

Yet that problem has been overcome, or forgotten, in com-mercial broadcasting. There the broadcasting organization, on radio or television, takes nothing from the listener or viewer. The sole revenue comes from the advertiser. Businessmen have been none the less willing to buy advertising space, and the public to respond to the advertisements and believe the information broadcast between them. The difference is one of the minor puzzles of the media. It follows presumably from practicalities. Newspapers are at least as easily sold as given away; a proportion of give-away sheets is thrown on the ground at once; whereas no satisfactory way of selling broadcast signals has ever been devised. Licence-fee systems are widely evaded, coin-in-the-slot devices are crushingly complicated to run on a large scale. Advertisements are so much the easiest way of financing broadcasting that they have made head even in non-capitalist countries.

Commercial broadcasters know no other system, and ask for none. Newspapermen, on the other hand, inheriting Northcliffe's vague doubts, often look for other means to money. The most obvious recourse would be to go back to the days before Northcliffe and ask the customer to pay something near what the paper cost to produce, instead of half of that or less. It would mean a steep rise in price. For years that was held to be suicidally bad for sales. Then in the 1960s it began to be seriously considered. But the succession of price rises which followed was largely a response to inflation; and although sales were not much affected, neither was the relation between advertisement and sales revenues. The opportunity was gone. It could not be expected to return until prices were so generally stable again as to be free of legal controls. Yet if that time ever came, there might be an equally strong case for putting up advertising rates rather than the price at the newsagent's. By the mid-1970s the revenue from advertisements was still there, as a proportion of the whole; but the cost of the labour to print them, and of the paper they were printed on, had grown so great as to come near cancelling any benefit to the newspaper. It was even calculated that, on the popular newspapers, advertising represented a net loss.

In hard-nosed commercial terms, the answer to that would be that newspapers should carry a great deal less advertising than they do at present, and at much higher rates. But that would have its drawbacks, too. Advertising is not simply a device for financing newspapers, harmless at best. It can be positively useful. The days are gone when the Personal Column of *The Times* was read for its value as entertainment; they disappeared when classified advertisements were demoted from the front page of *The Times* in May 1966. But small advertisements of that kind can help the private citizen sell cherished property, or find work, or choose a holiday. Display advertising enables companies to announce their results to shareholders, and Governments to set out the details of rearranged family allowances. It allows friends of the Arabs to inveigh against Israel, and friends of the environment to denounce nuclear power stations; and no journalist interferes.

Broadcast advertisements cannot claim quite the same degree of social usefulness; but local commercial radio, in particular, lets shops announce their sales weeks and special offers; and television can be a suitable medium for official exhortations about saving water or preventing fires.

The doubts persist. There is an unmistakable tension, in the press and broadcasting, between advertisements and the matter which surrounds them. The aim of journalism, broadly speaking, is to inform; sometimes to entertain; and if to persuade, then to persuade by an appeal to reason. The aim of advertisements is almost always to persuade, and to do it if need be by appealing to the least admirable impulses of the human mind, to envy and lust and insecurity. The measure of journalism is truth; the measure of advertising is effectiveness, and no more of the truth need appear than serves that purpose.

So the two have an air of being uneasy companions. It may well be that people who admire advertising, and know the case for its being the indispensable lubricant of commerce, are irked by its enforced association with journalism – all that foreign or financial coverage which may cause the bored eye to miss a vital advertisement, all that news of doom and disaster discouraging a buying mood. The irritation would be perfectly defensible. Believers in journalism are sometimes similarly troubled by its obligatory union with advertising. They fear contamination by advertising's different values.

They fear that advertisers, or the wish to please them, will deflect journalists from disclosing the truth as they know it, and that editorial matter will be changed or left out as a result. In general this is an unreal fear. Important cases where it may have happened are few and vague; cases where it has not are many and clear. Cigarette-makers are heavy advertisers in newspapers, and used to be on television until their advertisements were disallowed in August 1965; newspapers and broadcast news bulletins have always made prominent room for evidence that smoking can be lethal. Reports of the bad effects of alcoholism (notably in Scotland) have not been stinted; yet liquor firms have continued to advertise. The newspaper campaign against the slow payment of compensation to children maimed by thalidomide was not inhibited by the fact that Distillers were big newspaper advertisers. In July 1976 the asbestos industry, attacked on the ground that working with asbestos could cause a form of cancer, defended itself in a full-page advertisement in the *Sunday Times*; in the same issue, two staff reporters gave reasons for dissenting from several of the advertisement's claims. Much City journalism, published on pages hung about with advertisements for City institutions, is sharply critical of City ethics as well as of specific companies. Consumer journalism generally, broadcast and printed, examines advertised products with a developed scepticism.

The BBC bears its part in this work, but a smaller part than many newspapers. Yet the BBC has learnt to compete; if freedom from advertisements conferred extra boldness the BBC would show it. The fact is that advertisers are not much of an inhibition. Their interests are too dispersed. A national newspaper or broadcasting organization accommodates so many advertisers that the leverage any one of them can bring to bear is trifling. The largest advertiser on *The Times* contributes less than one half of one per cent to the paper's total revenue.

Another useful insulator from advertising matter is journalistic organization itself. Most journalists have nothing at all to do with the process which pays the bulk of their salaries. They never even meet their own colleagues in the advertising departments, let alone the advertisers themselves. But there are exceptions, in certain kinds of journalism. The necessary insulation is sometimes found to be a little perished.

It happens in journalism about women's clothes. Fashion writers have been known to mention a shop which advertises in their paper and ignore one which does not. The fusion of editorial with advertising interests is sometimes more subtle. Fashion magazines have a word for the result: aditorial. It describes words and pictures which purport to be of the journal's own free devising, but where much of the editorial cost – transport of models and photographer to an exotic location, for example – is borne by the firms whose clothes are being recommended. It can happen in travel articles, too, or pieces about wine.

Again, advertisers are sometimes able to persuade unwise newspapers to set an advertisement in the same type, or give it the same general appearance, as the rest of the newspaper. Advertisers like it, because the advertisement seems to borrow some of the credibility as fact which the paper's news columns claim. Newspapers ought to resist it, because it risks making the rest of the paper no more believable than advertising copy.

The seepage of advertising influence into the editorial columns is most marked in the advertising supplements which newspapers publish from time to time. At their best these supplements provide information about an industry, or a part of the world, which deserves detailed public notice and does not get it. But it is a condition of their being published that they should attract enough advertising to pay their costs and leave something over; and it is easy for them to be used as devices for drawing advertisements out of specialist companies and banks which would not ordinarily offer them. At their worst they can become mere advertisement-horses, like the advertising magazines which were removed from commercial television after Pilkington.

Even that is harmless enough, if the matter between the advertisements is as honest as the writers know how to make it. In March 1970 *The Times* proposed to publish a sixteen-page supplement about Hungary. The Hungarian Government was prepared to advertise. It asked to see the editorial matter first. The request was refused. The Hungarians withdrew their promise of advertising. That meant that the supplement would be unprofitable. It did not appear. The principle of unmanipulated truth was upheld.

Nevertheless, if the editorial matter was important, then the world was the poorer for its cancellation; and if it was not important, the *The Times* ought not to have proposed publication in the first place. These are areas of journalism where, even though the matter itself is sound, the decision to publish is not taken on plain journalistic grounds. It is a function of the supply of advertising. There are other such areas. Two notable ones are the coverage of business and motoring, which greatly increased during the 1960s. So did colour-supplement journalism. They expanded because newspaper managements established that advertising would be available to support the expansion; and editorial budgets were duly adjusted for the purpose. It is perfectly respectable to argue that the increased pool of available advertising accurately reflected an increased public interest. The editorial decisions were therefore taken for good journalistic reasons. But there may well have been other sides of life in which public interest was also rising: books, for example, or the theatre. Publishers and theatre managements were in no position to pay for more advertising than before. The editorial space made over to their concerns remained the same.

The wider charge, that editorial judgements are in general coarsened by the need for advertising, is harder to sustain. It is true that advertisers want to reach as many people as possible of a chosen kind. The more of those people a newspaper or a broadcasting organization can undertake to reach, the more it can charge the advertiser (and the more resources it will then have for doing its job efficiently). The work of journalists is thus coloured by the understanding that the larger the audience is, the better. Yet newspapermen have long been bound upon that wheel: part of a newspaper's income already comes direct from readers, and will increase as they do. It is true that advertising doubles the price on each new reader's head: he is precious not just for himself but for the increase in advertising rates he makes possible. But there is not much a newspaperman can do to differentiate a double from a single dose of zeal to attract new readers. Commercial broadcasters, after all, live off advertisers alone, and the BBC off listeners and viewers alone, and – in the years since competition was established – their methods of going after fresh income have not been very different.

The truth is that all journalists want as wide a hearing as possible. They would want it even in a country where there was a single newspaper and a single broadcasting station, both State-owned. There is very little point in publication unless you reach your public. But journalists also know that going after a wide audience entails certain sacrifices. General ideas are to be sparingly deployed. Recapitulation must be kept short. Exposition should be lightened with illustration, for the mind and the eye. The grave has to be relieved by the trivial. Appeal must be made to the impulses as well as the mind.

These rules are not necessarily coarsening. They are technical requirements to be overcome and used, like the rule that a sonnet must have fourteen lines. If blame is in point, it belongs not to any system of financing journalism but to human nature. Most people's minds are lazy, capricious, shy of abstract ideas, mildly prurient and soon bored. Journalists know that perfectly well, from their own. It remains the principal reason why their work is no better than it is.

Advertising is not an ideal source of finance. Although it alters the journalist's predicament little, it is not often an ornament. If newspapers take pride in exposing the risks of smoking, they cannot draw much satisfaction from continuing to carry cigarette advertisements. The Advertising Standards Authority, a body funded by the advertising industry itself, operates a detailed Code of Advertising Practice: 'Advertisements for anti-perspirants should not make exaggerated claims to keep skin dry either absolutely, or for a specific period', and so on. But the Authority cannot conceivably attempt to see all newspaper advertisements before they are published, and a good many questionable ones get under its net. The IBA, with enormous labour, does see all television-advertisement scripts in advance: in a recent year it examined 11,500. It measures them against its own code, and asks for changes in about a quarter of them. Yet no set of rules is entirely satisfactory. The IBA's code has been able to prevent advertisements from showing children eating sweets on the way to bed, but it has also disallowed televised appeals by charities (on the implausible ground that there is a finite pool of charitable money to be had, and wealthy charities would scoop it). No rules could have prevented a great many advertisements, particularly on television, from inducing a sense of dissatisfaction with the viewer's own circumstances and personality. Many an ordinarily harassed mother will have felt a pang at sight of a neat figure in a handsome kitchen receiving every fresh piece of negligence from her children with a tolerant smile.

Economically, advertisements have the disadvantage that they are the first thing a company cuts back when times are bad. Newspapers and commercial broadcasting organizations are thus among the first sufferers in a recession. That can be defended: an industry not supplying a necessity of life, nor adding appreciably to the foreign currency earnings with which necessities of life can be bought, is thus kept from taking an unwarranted share of the nation's resources. The fluctuation in advertisement volume, and therefore in numbers of pages or hours of fresh programming, and therefore in jobs, is nevertheless a nuisance to people seeking to buy the necessities of life with what they earn as print workers or broadcasting technicians or journalists.

For newspapers, the central fact about advertisement finance is that it is most richly bestowed on those who need it least. Given a choice between two newspapers addressing the same kind of people, the advertiser will choose the paper which sells the more copies. With the extra money, the preferred paper will improve its service and win still more readers from its rival. In the end, the rival will starve to death. It almost happened to the *Observer*, overshadowed by the *Sunday Times*, in August 1975; and it did happen to the *Star*, the London evening paper which closed in October 1960. At the end the *Star* was still selling more copies than the *Evening Standard*; but it sold many fewer than the *Evening News* to the working-class readers who were its chosen market, and the *News* took its advertising away.

In part this is no more than the ordinary law of life, remarked on in St Matthew's Gospel if not before, that success is rewarded and failure punished. Nor is it necessarily a bad thing: resources are put into the hands of those who have shown they know how to use them. But the newspaper business is not like other forms of commerce. A paper can fall behind a rival because it prefers to address intellect rather than emotion, or because it reserves the best of its coverage for areas of no great popular appeal, like foreign affairs or the arts. Unsuccessful newspapers are not always bad ones; and bad or not, they help supply the diversity which the press must maintain if it is to do its job. If the system of advertisement finance worsens the problems of unsuccessful papers, it is not wholly healthy.

For that reason there have been recurrent suggestions that advertising revenue should be limited or evened out. (Three such schemes were considered and rejected by the Shawcross Commission in September 1962.) The point of limiting advertisement revenue would be to restrict the distance by which success might draw ahead of failure. It could be done by putting a statutory limit on the proportion of its space which a paper might make over to advertising, or by taxing gross advertising revenue above a certain figure. The first device would give the State a stout new lever with which to shift its principal critics; and both would impoverish the industry as a whole, and diminish such capacity for excellence as it has. Thoughts have therefore turned to schemes for equalizing revenue.

The simplest way would be to share it. Since rich newspapers would not share their wealth with poorer rivals unless they were compelled to, the agency of the State is again called in. The proposal appeared in its most developed form in a Labour party study group report published in June 1974 under the title *The People and the Media* (and broadly approved at the party's October 1975 conference). The report suggested founding an Advertising Revenue Board: it would set each newspaper's advertising rates, collect the advertiser's money, keep part of it to help poor papers with their newsprint buying and part for grants to start new papers, and redistribute the rest among other newspapers by the light of an undetermined formula.

Political objections aside for a moment, the scheme has practical difficulties. Newspapers would lose all incentive to work hard at getting advertisement business. Total advertisement revenue would go down. There would be very little to spare for new or weak publications. Yet costs would go up, because the appearance or survival of these nurselings would increase the demand for newsprint and push up its price. As a result there would be a lot of feeble newspapers, and no forceful ones.

An alternative is to seek to level up rather than level down – to inject new money, which would be public money, into the budgets of weak newspapers until their advertising revenue attained a certain level. A form of this idea was proposed by Professor Fred Hirsch of Warwick University and David Gordon of the *Economist* in a book published in May 1975 called *Newspaper Money* (Hutchinson). Their aim was the specialized but laudable one of seducing readers away from the popular to the quality papers; and in order to persuade non-popular newspapers 'to go further down-market than would otherwise be profitable' (p. 126), they suggested an Exchequer bounty of £10 an extra reader a year. The bounty would tail off as the paper's advertising revenue rose with its circulation, and would stop altogether when it reached three-quarters of a paper's total income.

The plan assumed that it was possible to attract working-class readers in significant numbers by reflecting working-class political concerns. In this century and last, countless newspapers have tried that and failed. But the root objection to both these schemes is that they admit the State – the proper object of press criticism – into a position of power within the management of the press. In the Labour study group's scheme, the State would have the enormous overall power of deciding which papers to fund and which not; and it would be remarkable if newspapers unfriendly to the Government in power were as considerately treated as papers which supported it. More, a newspaper's advertising rates are central to its whole commercial policy. It would be very difficult for the State to set them without becoming involved in the management of individual newspapers, including the negotiation of editorial budgets.

The Hirsch-Gordon plan avoids those grosser pitfalls. But the mere fact of the bounty's being paid, and therefore the possibility of its being cut off, would give the Government a hold over just those newspapers which would otherwise be most likely to publish disclosures damaging to it; and the power to vary the level of advertising revenue at which the bounty was diminished or withdrawn would equip ministers with a finely adjustable weapon to use against papers which displeased them.

It is a pity that advertising has come to be as important a source of finance as it has. But it was inevitable that newspapers should be used for advertising almost from the first; and once goods could be produced in great quantities, and newspapers (and later broadcasting) reached a mass market, advertising was bound to become a major source of media finance. It then grew into a force for lessening the number of newspapers, and so their diversity. For people who believe that the State is sufficient guardian of the citizen's interests and liberties, there may be forms of State intervention which could correct that. For those who believe that the State's capacity to do evil is greater than the capacity of private citizens or bodies, there are none.

Chapter 6: Unions

Over against the influences representing capital – the owners, the advertisers – stand the organizations representing labour: the trade unions. They are not in origin concerned with the control of the media; and yet their activities bear on it, indirectly and directly.

Printers have been a distinct fraternity so long that their private term for the fellowship in which they work – chapel – has been known since the end of the seventeenth century; and even then it was so old that its derivation was disputed. (The general belief is that it comes from William Caxton's having set up the first English print-shop, two centuries before that, in the precincts of Westminster Abbey.) Strike action by printers was threatened at least as early as 1786 (against the founder of *The Times*, John Walter, for hiring an extra apprentice in his book-printing house); and it was regularly taken throughout the nineteenth century, well before the rights of unions were defined. So by the time mass production and the twentieth century arrived together, newspaper printers were well placed to use their industrial muscle. They had had plenty of practice; their product was valuable and perishable, which made managements ready to pay to avoid stoppages; and the demands of the trade made print workers intelligent and disciplined men.

The core of their union activity remained what it had been from the first: guarding their own jobs. In this they were famously successful. By November 1966 the Economist Intelligence Unit's survey of the national newspaper industry (Part IV, pp. 60–1) could say of newspaper production:

Manning standards are usually set by horse trading, and often bear little relationship to the needs of the job . . . Many departments are heavily overmanned, and there will clearly be major problems in reducing this over-manning without serious hardship.

Success proved self-defeating. Manning levels which had been tolerable in good times began to seem a threat to certain newspapers' survival by the middle 1970s, when Fleet Street was troubled by national recession (which limited advertising), worldwide inflation (which pushed the cost of paper steadily upwards), and recurrent industrial disputes (which held back production and therefore revenue). In December 1976 a report to the McGregor Commission confirmed the overmanning on the evidence of the unions themselves, and ascribed the disputes to 'sectionalism' – rivalry between different unions and to some extent between different managements (*Industrial Relations in the National Newspaper Industry*: A Report by the Advisory Conciliation and Arbitration Service, cmnd 6680, pars. 644–66). That certainly encouraged pay claims, and disunity among employers in dealing with them; but a deeper cause was the failure of big newspapers to breed any corporate commitment in the mass of their workforce, any sense of the importance of the product.

Yet that was a problem shared with much of the rest of industry, and no more amenable to swift change than recession or inflation; whereas overmanning, it turned out, might be. The opportunity arose from a proffered revolution in printing methods. The last big change had been in 1884, when Ottmar Mergenthaler (a German immigrant to the United States) invented the Linotype machine. It casts a molten lead alloy into solid lines of type. They are arranged by compositors in a page-shaped metal frame; from it is taken an impression in papier mâché, and a semi-cylindrical metal casting made from the impression is clamped to the rotary presses. In the early 1960s a new technique emerged in the United States. It replaces the Linotype machine with a photocomposition machine, producing a printed image by photography. Journalists' words are typed direct into a computer. The computer stores them, registers corrections, straightens the margins and sends the result to the photo-composition machine. The machine itself, or a scissors-and-paste operation on its output, produces a printed page; and a photograph of the page is turned into a plastic half-cylinder for the presses. In principle, therefore, the new process saves the labour of Linotype operators, compositors and proof-readers.

By March 1976 most Fleet Street newspapers were considering which makes of machine to buy; the interim McGregor report had recommended that they should have Government help in borrowing money both to pay for the equipment and to compensate men who lost their jobs; and leaders of the main print unions were talking to the Newspaper Publishers' Association about how the change-over should be arranged. During the year it became evident that both perfecting the equipment and accustoming large numbers of union members to the idea of being bought out of their jobs would take years rather than months; but the process was in train.

The bearing of these moves on the question of newspaper control was that they prevented its being raised. The new technology of printing was a fresh start. The machines were expensive, but no more expensive for a new management than an old, and cheaper to run than the hot-metal process because of lower wage bills. In principle, the development of cold-type printing made founding a new newspaper easier than it had been before.

The unions were not interested. The disappearance of even one newspaper would have made an opening for a paper differently controlled. But to preserve as many of their members' jobs as possible, they chose to save as many existing newspapers as they could; and if that committed them to preserving an existing pattern of newspaper ownership, and with it an existing order of society, they seemed not to notice it as a problem.

Another way for unions to change the pattern of newspaper

101

control is to go into ownership themselves. It has been done. For the seven years before the 1929 deal with Odhams, the main owner of the *Daily Herald* was the TUC; and it kept a 49 per cent shareholding till the paper's end in 1964. The idea of union proprietorship was revived by a number of union leaders in the 1970s. The moving spirit was Bill Keys, General Secretary of one of the print unions, SOGAT (the Society of Graphical and Allied Trades). He said in an August 1976 statement:

> I have long been conscious of the gap in our national newspaper scene created by the disappearance of the *Daily Herald* and the *News Chronicle*. We do not want to resurrect either of those two papers, but to provide an independent daily of the Labour movement, able to present the news without the political bias of private ownership, yet free to criticize the TUC or the party.
>
> There has been a growing concentration towards the right in the press over the last decade, and that is recognized by executives in Fleet Street. We are not getting the current reflection of the middle and left ground in politics. So there is a need for a paper that can do this.

Yet it was clear from the instinctive scepticism of other union chiefs that the idea was a good way from realization. The problem could no longer be disguised as a commercial one. Part of the *Herald*'s problem, admittedly, had been that it was unattractive to advertisers. Although it was still selling more than a million copies a day when it closed, its readers were both less numerous than the *Express*'s or the *Mail*'s and poorer; and they were much poorer than readers of papers like the *Guardian*, to which the *Herald* offered a half-hearted intellectual challenge. Twelve years later, though, differences in real income between, say, a fitter and a teacher had been noticeably diminished. Advertisers would know that, and would be happier than they had been before to address the readers of a union-owned newspaper.

There would still remain the rest of the *Herald*'s difficulty: shortage of readers. In 1932 it became the first newspaper in the world to announce a sale of 2 million copies a day. Three years before, the circulation had been little more than a quarter of a million. But the new readers had been bought, not persuaded. After the 1929 deal the *Herald* was still the organ of a serious political movement. The methods which in the later 1930s took the *Mirror* to a sale of over 4 million – strip cartoons, garish presentation, a heavy reliance on crime and sex – were not therefore open to the *Herald*. Julius Elias, chairman of Odhams (and later Lord Southwood), went after readers for it another way. He bribed them with presents. An army of 50,000 canvassers was recruited at £3 a week to go from door to door and drum up custom. People who signed a promise to become registered readers for ten weeks were rewarded with the luxuries of those days: fountain pens, silk stockings, sets of fish knives and forks.

Even on those terms, the *Herald* could not keep its lead. The *Express* felt impelled to fight back with fish knives of its own. The *Mail* and the *News Chronicle* followed a little behind. The cost was crippling. At a meeting of newspaper owners, Elias had to agree to a ban on outright gifts. But Odhams was also a publishing house, and had found a cheap book-binding process. Elias could offer sets of Dickens's novels at a very low price which nevertheless covered their cost. Beaverbrook, at the *Express*, promised war to the death with the same weapons. He offered sets of Dickens at a price below cost. The *Herald* had barely passed the magic 2 million mark before the *Express* overhauled it and drew away. The race was ended by the Second World War; and after it the *Herald*'s circulation fell steadily.

The paper's real difficulty, in sum, was that readers were not drawn to it for itself. Its natural public, who needed it and whom it needed, was the category of serious-minded Labour voters. There were not enough of them. The insufficiency was no reflection on the merit of the Labour cause. If anything, it uncovered a limitation of the written word. Attentive reading requires silence; ideally, solitude. Silence and solitude are most easily had by the comfortably off. But Labour voters are not for the most part comfortably off; and neither, as a consequence, is a newspaper that addresses them. Trade unionists were aware of all that. The union movement did little to help the co-operative experiment at the *Scottish Daily News*; it was in no hurry to undertake any new venture in newspaper publishing.

That has not stopped groups of union members from occasionally seeking to wield control over newspapers by another means: industrial action. There was a run of incidents in 1970 and 1971 when newspaper workers were moved by editorial matter they disliked to interfere with a newspaper's production. SOGAT members had a letter about overmanning in Fleet Street taken out of the *Observer*. NATSOPA (the National Society of Operative Printers, Graphical and Media Personnel) obliged the same newspaper, under threat of a stoppage, first to shelve a report of a dispute between printing unions and the next week to run it with a NATSOPA reply alongside. The federated house chapel at the *Evening Standard* stopped the presses there until a late edition because print workers objected to a cartoon about a power workers' dispute then in course: the union principally engaged in it, the Electrical Trades Union, had members at the *Standard*. At the Bristol *Evening Post*, NATSOPA members refused to print the last edition because they disputed the paper's report of a lunch-time rally they had held to protest against the Heath Government's Industrial Relations Bill, then going through Parliament. The Southend *Evening Echo* missed a day's print when NATSOPA members, at the instance of the local Transport and General Workers' branch secretary, objected to the paper's publishing a ballot form for use in a strike at the Ford car factory nearby.

In the last incident of the series, the *Scottish Daily Express* lost a large part of its edition in an argument over a cartoon which suggested that the IRA had Russian help. This row was untypical. Prime movers in it were members of the NUJ (to the displeasure of their union's National Executive); and the field of dispute was international politics. In the other stoppages the complainants were print workers, not journalists, and the matter complained of had to do with industrial affairs.

It was at any rate an area where the workers could claim a certain expertise. Indeed, all the items which gave offence were about disputes of which the offended union members had a measure of direct knowledge. So they were not relying on any general belief that, in capitalist-owned newspapers, a strike report unfavourable to the strikers is likely to be unfair. Further, the power they used was not new. There had long been censorship of labour news about newspapers. Print workers had not had to apply it themselves; journalists did it for them, out of fear of what the print workers would do otherwise. When journalists advanced in boldness, print workers made the threat actual.

There was a recrudescence of the same trouble in January 1977, when members of the National Graphical Association stopped *The Times* rather than print as it stood a report of an article published elsewhere by David Astor, the recently retired editor of the *Observer*, which looked back over his industrial difficulties there. Yet the movement was unlikely to go far. The world is too complicated to let it. When the item at issue is not about labour news, the journalist has the edge. The Linotype operator who sets a story about schools, for example, and the van-driver who carries the paper which contains it to the station, are likely to have at least as firm a view about schooling as the paper's education correspondent. But they would rapidly find that they were no match for him in argument, because he spends his day hearing or reading relevant evidence, and they do not. The growing extent to which workers take part in the running of their firm's affairs, even if backed by statute, cannot alter that.

Discussion serves only to set differences in knowledge in a sharper light.

In television, true, that check has been less inhibiting. The main union for the non-journalistic staff of television companies, the Association of Cinematograph, Television and Allied Technicians (ACTT), has been led by men of pronounced political views. ACTT made no attempt to become a shareholder in commercial television at the times when franchises were being distributed. But it has shown occasional interest in wielding editorial control. It has imposed bans on television filming in South Africa and Greece; and they have been more or less observed.

This comparatively effective activism follows from the fact that television technicians are on the whole better educated than print workers, and that television journalism is anyway a more broad-brush, eclectic operation than newspaper work. There is never a lack of disordered countries to make television programmes about; a choice has to be made; and a television company will have few journalists on its staff who can present a detailed case for choosing one country rather than another. So union wishes can be painlessly met. But that has not been ACTT's main thrust. Its chief interest is still in protecting the jobs and living standards of its members; and with certain commercial television companies it has made agreements which are more limiting than any political resolution. If a film crew must number seven people for a job which has sometimes been done by two, and if they must all travel first-class on journeys of more than a thousand miles, then that is itself a sufficient reason not to film in South Africa. It is an equally strong reason not to film in the United States, Russia or whatever countries the union believes viewers ought to see. As long as that attitude persists, ACTT leaders cannot be thought to make editorial influence a prime aim. They would prefer to take the material solaces instead.

The people who have most often pooled their strength in order to secure editorial ends have been journalists of the written word. The most striking cases have concerned the appointment of editors. Between April 1972 and November 1975 the *New Statesman*, the *Guardian* and the *Observer* all had occasion to find new ones. Each time, staff journalists were able – either by ensuring that they were directly consulted, or through the use of a veto – to wield decisive influence on the choice.

The practice is not as entirely laudable as it may at first seem. On each paper, the new editor was chosen from among his colleagues. He was therefore predominantly in their image: youngish, conciliatory and male. There were no retired politicians, no eccentric autocrats, no women. Three opportunities to extend the press's necessary diversity were lost. Moreover, the gain in staff power was not without corresponding loss. Because an editor had forfeited something of his sovereignty, so had his staff members: he could no longer protect them. A journalist who offered unfashionable opinions on a sensitive subject like race or schooling, or even who reported unwelcome facts about them, might find the collective weight of his colleagues used against him; and the editor, depending on the same influence to keep his job, could offer no protection. The offending matter would be excluded.

On the other hand, it can be argued that to allow the staff a veto, or even a positive power of election, is no more than to formalize an already existing state of affairs. A newspaper is a committee in permanent but fragmented session. Journalists are for ever at grips with their superiors over matters of editorial judgement – urging them to cover this story rather than that, to carry a leader on this topic rather than that. Much of this advice is taken. In general, a paper's distinctive tone is set as much by its staff as by its editor. If an editor is not in tune with his staff, the paper's energy will be dissipated in quarrels and its characteristic note will no longer be heard. The neatest way to see that editor and journalists are at one is to give them a voice in his appointment.

The arrangement to be avoided is one which leaves the editor so dependent on the staff's continuing goodwill as to put him virtually at their orders. If that happens, then the result is the familiar consequence of anarchy: everyone's freedom is diminished, because there is no one to protect it.

Yet that was exactly the effect feared from a change in the law which had a contentious passage through Parliament between April 1974 and March 1976. It was brought in by Michael Foot, then Secretary of State for Employment. Its most notable aim was to restore legality to closed shops. A side effect, unintended by ministers at first and yet not much regretted once discovered, was to circumscribe the independence of editors.

A closed shop is a place of work where everyone must belong, either as a condition or as a consequence of being taken on, to a certain trade union. Unions like the device, since it gives them strength in industrial bargaining; and managements, too, are often content to have a single team on the other side of the table. The arrangement had nevertheless been outlawed as a potential tyranny over the individual worker in the Heath Government's Industrial Relations Act of 1971. But that Government had been brought down over a dispute with the National Union of Mineworkers. The premise of Labour's limited victory in February 1974 was that a Labour Government would restore good relations between the unions and the State. An important gesture to that end was to license closed shops again.

The task was first attempted in the Trade Union and Labour Relations Bill, introduced in April 1974. The Conservative Opposition in the Commons sought to amend the Bill so as to allow a worker to refuse to join a particular union 'on any reasonable grounds', and to protect him if – once in a union – he lost his job through being expelled from it. The Government, having no overall majority in the Commons, lost certain votes which obliged it to accept the amendments, and the Bill went through in that weakened form. But after Labour had strengthened its hold on power in the October 1974 election, Foot renewed his original intention in a Trade Union and Labour Relations (Amendment) Bill.

Newspaper editors became increasingly worried about the effect the proposal might have in newspaper offices. The Government had not set out with the aim of indulging the National Union of Journalists. Yet if the second Bill became law as it stood, the NUJ could seek to establish a closed shop for journalists in any newspaper office. If the union succeeded, it could block the employment of non-union specialists – doctors, divines – as occasional writers. More than that, it could ask the editor to join. If he refused, that might provoke a stoppage which his employers could only end by dismissing him; and they would not need to pay him compensation. If – the likelier course, therefore – he joined, he might find himself at union orders about what he should publish or whom he should employ. The instructions would be enforceable by industrial action. They might come either from the chapel – the staff of the newspaper, by majority vote – or from the union nationally. Either way, the editor's freedom to publish minority views, even from among his own staff, would be endangered.

Both the Government and the unions were entitled to reply, as they did, that closed shops had been permitted for years before 1971, and none of these feared consequences had come about. Editors noted on the other side that the NUJ, like other collar-and-tie unions, had lately developed a new self-assertiveness, both at branch level and nationally. In 1965 it had forced an agreement with managements about the years of provincial service needed before a journalist might work in Fleet Street. Between 1970 and 1974 it had become increasingly restive over sports reporting by sportsmen rather than sports journalists. In a number of provincial disputes over pay during 1973 and 1974, NUJ members had as a negotiating tactic refused to handle material from non-members. In October 1974 the union had done away with the associate membership which gave a sheltered status to such editors and deputy editors as belonged to it.

The editors were right to raise a doubt. Intelligent choice in a democracy needs a free press, which in modern terms means media where all points of view can find written or broadcast expression. In practice, that cannot happen: there is not room. But there is a prospect that something like it will happen as long as there are enough different editors to make the choice from among the publishable material offered. Hence the importance of the principle of diversity. If it works properly, it provides that all points of view for which there is anything to be said at all are at least sampled. But that principle cannot be observed if editorial choice is in the end governed by the decisions of a single union, however public-spirited it is.

When the second Foot Bill was introduced in November 1974, Conservative and Liberal amendments concentrated on making the press an exception. The attempt failed in the Commons; but it succeeded for a while in the Lords. A pacific Labour peer, Lord Houghton, produced the idea of a charter of press freedom to be negotiated within the industry after the Bill was passed. Foot accepted it. Opposition and cross-bench peers wanted the charter's terms spelled out and made enforceable at law. With the session running out, and using their Lords majority, they persisted in carrying amendments to that effect.

Rather than accept them, Foot preferred to let the Bill drop and bring it forward again in the next session. The terms of the Parliament Acts of 1911 and 1949 kept the Lords from savaging it a second time. The Bill finally became an Act in March 1976. It had largely preserved its original form; but it included this passage (in section 2) marked 'Freedom of the press':

If before the end of the period of twelve months beginning with the passing of the Trade Union and Labour Relations (Amendment) Act 1976, there is agreed among parties including employers of journalists (or employers' associations representing such employers), editors (or editors' organizations) and trade unions representing journalists, a charter containing practical guidance for employers, trade unions and editors and other journalists on matters relating to the freedom of the press, the Secretary of State shall lay before both Houses of Parliament a draft of that charter.

Practical guidance on matters relating to the freedom of the press must include guidance on the avoidance of improper pressure to distort or suppress news, comment, or criticism, the application of union membership agreements to journalists (and in particular the right of editors to discharge their duties and to commission and to publish any article) and the question of access for contributors.

If no such charter was agreed, or if Parliament did not accept it when it was, the Secretary of State was to see where the parties had got to and work out one of his own. He could also revise it later at need. The charter would provide for a body to hear complaints under it, to pronounce on them and to have those pronouncements published. That was the limit of its force.

It was clear from the outset that the parties listed in the Act would find agreement impossible. Certain employers and editors thought it would be right to comply with the law and to put together what charter they could. Some thought the whole exercise pointless, since even if the charter were to define an editor's rights it could not guarantee them: it would not be enforceable in the courts. Others thought any charter damnable, on the ground that to define liberties in a statute is both to circumscribe them and to create the possibility that they can be diminished by a later statute. The BBC and the IBA were not disposed to enter the struggle at all: the editorial freedom of their news

111

operations was secured by other Acts, and anyway this Act did not mention broadcasting. Most important of all, there was very little chance of agreement between the two 'trade unions representing journalists' – the NUJ and the Institute of Journalists.

The IOJ had a membership a twelfth the size of the NUJ's. It was the older body, and historically it represented journalists who saw their work as a profession rather than a trade. But even without that difference of view, its position as the lesser union in nearly every newspaper office meant that it stood to be serially extinguished. Early in 1976, well before the Foot Bill became law, a branch of the NUJ in Barnsley had some success in persuading local trade union officials and Labour councillors not to give information to journalists who belonged to the IOJ. The move had the support of the NUJ's National Executive, and later of its annual conference, and was copied elsewhere. By June 1977, at least two NUJ branches seeking closed shops in provincial offices had forced the issue to a strike.

The NUJ, in truth, was unluckily placed. Its leaders, and the majority of its members, wanted it to function as an ordinary trade union; and yet it was not in an ordinary trade. They were understandably concerned that it should win good pay and conditions for its members. To that end, the closed shop was a useful device: the threat or fact of strike action by NUJ members would not then be nullified by the presence in the same office of other journalists who could do the work instead. Many NUJ people, particularly on provincial papers, felt their work to be a trade and nothing else. If Tennyson found it a 'sad, mechanic exercise' to write *In Memoriam*, checking the names at the funeral of a councillor could hardly be more.

The union was further encouraged in its stance by a great many Labour politicians and union leaders, starting with Foot, who had himself been an editor (of the *Evening Standard* and later of *Tribune*) in his time. But that very encouragement showed journalism to be a little different from other ways of making a living. These people were interested in the closed shop in newspaper offices for something more than its usefulness in industrial disputes. They looked forward to seeing a press which was sympathetic to the cause of Labour. They wanted the flow of information coloured a different way. The denial by NUJ leaders that their support for the closed shop had any bearing on press freedom, though honest in intention, was not altogether true in fact.

Journalists handle a public utility: information (including information about diverse opinion). They are on all fours with power workers or water engineers. There is a moral difficulty about the claim that they can take up the strike weapon with the same cheerful freedom as other groups of workers. A number of NUJ members perceived that. In London offices they were still in a majority, even though without the doubtful protection of a charter. (The talks had duly failed to produce one, and by the summer of 1977 there was no sign that Foot's successor as Employment Secretary, Albert Booth, was preparing to impose one.) The press remained an awkward field for unions to work in, whether their aim was political or merely material.

Chapter 7: The State

The media and the State – the whole apparatus of Government – are in two minds about each other. On the one hand, a certain tension separates them; on the other, undeniable ties bind them.

Antagonism between journalists and politicians is as old as the press itself; and it has been intensified by the coming of broadcasting. The classic statement of the reasons for it appeared in a leading article in *The Times* as long ago as 1852. *The Times* had been stern in its attacks on the cruelty of Louis Napoleon's new regime in France. Westminster opinion was afraid that the criticism would endanger Franco-British relations. Lord Derby, then Leader of the Opposition and soon to be Prime Minister, said in the Lords that 'If, as in these days, the press aspires to exercise the influence of statesmen, the press should remember that they are not free from the corresponding responsibility of statesmen.' *The Times*'s leader-writers replied on 6 February – in words which deserve to be set out again – that the purpose and duties of the 'two powers' were constantly separate and sometimes diametrically opposite.

The first duty of the press is to obtain the earliest and most correct intelligence of the time, and instantly, by disclosing them, to make them the common property of the nation . . . The press lives by disclosures; whatever passes into its keeping becomes a part of the knowledge and the history of our times; it is daily and for ever appealing to the enlightened force of public opinion – anticipating, if possible, the march of events – standing upon the breach between the present and the future, and extending its survey to the horizon of the world. The statesman's duty is precisely the reverse. He cautiously guards from the public eye the information by which his

actions and opinions are regulated; he reserves his
judgement on passing events till the latest moment, and
then he records it in obscure or conventional language;
he strictly confines himself, if he be wise, to the practical
interests of his own country, or to those bearing immediately upon it; he hazards no rash surmises as to
the future; and he concentrates in his own transactions
all that power which the press seeks to diffuse over the
world. The duty of the one is to speak; of the other to
be silent.

The Times pitched the case a little high. A Government
might in many circumstances govern the better and more
acceptably for speaking out. It could then look for guidance
and support from understanding voters. But the instinct
to governmental secrecy is old and deep. Sometimes there is
national value in it. If the Cabinet has settled on the best
offer it can make in a dispute over wages in a nationalized
industry, then the general interest is best served by keeping
the figure secret, since a settlement may be reached at a
lower figure and the State's money saved.

Sometimes, though, secrecy serves a narrower purpose.
If a Government is in process of deciding whether or not to
develop a hugely expensive new passenger aeroplane, and if
the real case for building it is not that it will make money
but that it will save jobs or preserve an alliance, then the
ministers and civil servants engaged will want nothing
said until the decision has been safely taken, since otherwise
the public voice might be raised against that kind of short-
term reasoning. Disclosure in the press or on the air that
Whitehall is discussing the question, and in what terms, will
then be for the general good. Later revelation that the decision was in fact made for unsound or even corrupt reasons
would be less useful, but it might still stop the same thing
happening again.

Besides dragging fact into the open, journalists may also
bring forward unwelcome argument. Politicians, dependent

on the voters' favour, hope that public comment on their plans and deeds will be favourable. Newspapermen writing leaders or opinion pieces about those decisions are not much concerned with that. They have blind spots of their own; but they go through the motions, at any rate, of championing objective wisdom. So even if they conclude that the Government is on balance right, they cannot avoid marshalling the considerations on the other side.

This tension between journalists and politicians has been given a new twist by the development of broadcasting. For many years, broadcasting the spoken word was a matter of reading the written word aloud. When politicians broadcast, they had a script. During the 1950s and 1960s, though, there was a steady shift from the script to the unrehearsed interview. It followed partly from television's need for a regularly changing picture, partly from a belief that television had a gift for disclosing character and that this was the way to exploit it, partly from the feeling that an arrangement where one person talked while everybody else shut up and listened belonged with a stratified order of society which had passed away. The device also saves a busy man's time: talking is less trouble than writing, and few politicians are prepared to concede that it is a less precise instrument. Both Harold Wilson and James Callaghan were content, even when they had an important thought to put to the nation, to explain it on television to an interviewer rather than straight to a camera.

Now an interviewer cannot simply ask 'And what is your next point?' – unless the conversation is to appear dull and unnatural. The questions he can most plausibly ask are about the things which people at large might not understand or might disagree with. The practice has become established that the interviewer voices the doubts. Many of them are queries which the plain voter might not have thought of unaided. Often politicians find them unfair. But the development was unavoidable. The result is that broadcast journalism regularly presents reasons for dissenting from a Government decision in the very act of reporting it.

Yet there are many points at which journalism and the State have common interests. The State provides the framework of law without which journalism could not operate. Representatives of the State are the actual owners of the BBC, and might one day own other news organizations besides. Government in all its branches is a principal theme of news journalism, and its greatest single source of information; and the business of governing, reciprocally, would be impossible without newspapers and broadcasting stations to expound it. The State, finally, claims the loyalty of individual journalists as citizens.

The point about the framework of law applies particularly to broadcasting. Newspapers profit from the fact that their contracts with their suppliers are enforceable at law, and that (except in Northern Ireland) their delivery vans are not hijacked on the streets; but so do all businesses. Broadcasting needs extra help. In order that the ether shall not be a babel of conflicting sounds, there has to be a central authority, recognized nationally and internationally, which decides who shall broadcast on what frequencies. In practice the job can be done only by an agency of the State. In the United Kingdom it has been done successively by the Post Office and the Home Office, with certain powers over commercial broadcasting delegated to a Government-appointed body, the Independent Broadcasting Authority. The IBA, and hence the State, also owns the transmitters which commercial broadcasters use. At the BBC, State participation goes further yet. Not merely is the Corporation itself and all its equipment publicly owned, through its governors, but the State is its revenue-collector: licence fees are gathered in through post offices.

Inevitably, these arrangements give the State certain powers over broadcasting. Politicians have felt entitled to demand something in return – at any rate for emergency use. The powers are written into the legal instruments which give the BBC and the IBA conditional permission to organize broadcasts. The BBC's Licence and Agreement (as restated in July 1969, when ministerial responsibility for broadcasting had not yet passed to the Home Secretary – clause 13, sections 3 and 4) gives the Government these very wide powers:

> The Corporation shall, whenever so requested by any Minister of Her Majesty's Government in the United Kingdom at the Corporation's own expense, send from all or any of the stations any announcement (with a visual image of any picture or object mentioned in the announcement if it is sent from the television stations or any one of them) which such Minister may request the Corporation to broadcast; and shall also, whenever so requested by any such Minister in whose opinion an emergency has risen or continues, at the like expense send as aforesaid any other matter which such Minister may request the Corporation to broadcast; Provided that the Corporation when sending such an announcement or other matter may at its discretion announce or refrain from announcing that it is sent at the request of a named Minister.
>
> The Postmaster General may from time to time by notice in writing require the Corporation to refrain at any specified time or at all times from sending any matter or matters of any class specified in such notice; and the Postmaster General may at any time or times vary or revoke any such notice. The Corporation may at its discretion announce or refrain from announcing that such a notice has been given or has been varied or revoked.

The BBC may explain that it is under duress, but it cannot escape the duress. It is subject to Government directive about hours of broadcasting (clause 14); and it is also required, in a memorandum attached to the Licence, 'to refrain from expressing its own opinion on current affairs or on matters of public policy'. The same injunctions have applied to commercial broadcasting from its beginnings. (In the Independent Broadcasting Authority Act 1973 they appear as sections 4, 21 and 22.)

It can be argued that these powers are purely for emergency use; and certainly they have been little used. But the State's instructions to the BBC go further. Two burdens are laid on it (in clause 13 of the Licence, sections 2 and 5) which commercial broadcasting escapes:

The Corporation shall broadcast an impartial account day by day prepared by professional reporters of the proceedings in both Houses of the United Kingdom Parliament.

The Corporation shall send programmes in the External Services to such countries, in such languages and at such times as, after consultation with the Corporation, may from time to time be prescribed . . .

Those obligations are regularly met. So the BBC, State-owned and discharging special services for the State, shows signs of being at the State's orders. Certainly a good many politicians have that impression. Convinced of the importance of having television on their side, and reasoning that if the Government has given the BBC a licence it can in theory take it away again, politicians often expect the BBC to subserve the ruling regime – or at the very least the reigning system of morality. The BBC, aware that its national and international prestige is such that its licence could never be taken away altogether, demurs. It knows (though it does not say so in so many words) that reigning parties and orthodoxies change, and ought to change, and that broadcasts which always sustained them would not necessarily be for the good of the nation as a whole. For a quiet life, its servants sometimes draw back from a decision which they know

119

would give offence: they decide not after all to have a political party represented in a studio discussion by a known maverick, not to broadcast an interview with a declared enemy of the forces of order. But in general they believe that, except in time of emergency, the BBC should work to its own choices and not the Government's.

The result is a state of recurrent bad relations between the Corporation and any party which is in office or might be. Commercial broadcasters, on the other hand, inhabit a calmer world. Since they are not so clearly part of a State chain, politicians expect less of them; and they themselves are more sensitive to the anticipated reactions of powerful people. For commercial broadcasters, the threat of losing their franchise to broadcast is not an empty one. It has happened to some of them (notably in the 1967 Hill reshuffle). They are prepared to temper their public spirit with commercial prudence.

Newspapermen are luckier than broadcasters. Aside from the ordinary protection of the law, there is no State help which is indispensable to them. They can fix their territories by plain commercial decision; they have their distribution and revenue-collection done by a host of private enterprises – wholesalers, newsagents, advertising agencies. The State has had very little part in the newspaper business since the lapse of licensing at the end of the seventeenth century and the lifting of stamp duties in the middle of the nineteenth.

Stamp duties were in part a postal subsidy; and it is true that postal subsidies continue. The Post Office calculated that, during 1975, 12 million national newspapers carrying second-class stamps were delivered by postmen as first-class mail. But 12 million twopences (the difference between the two rates) amounted to no more than £240,000 – not an annual sum whose withdrawal would bring the press to its knees. The various concessionary printed-paper rates to places abroad applied as much to books or advertising matter or correspondence-course material as they did to

newspapers and magazines, and represented for the Post
Office a straightforward commercial speculation.

The other concession made by the State looked more
substantial. When the United Kingdom introduced Value
Added Tax in April 1973, it did not join certain other
member countries of the European Economic Community
in applying the tax to newspapers. By 1975 the remission
was worth £20 million a year to national newspapers. In
lean times it was a sum they were glad not to have to find.
On the other hand, the power of imposing new taxes is
one which Governments hold over all enterprises all the
time. The threat is too generalized and permanent to have
any practical effect on conduct.

So the State does not have the peculiar sway over newspapers that it has over broadcasting. But there are recurrent
suggestions that it should. They are not made with State
influence in mind; yet that would be their consequence.
The People and the Media, the Labour party's 1974 pamphlet,
proposed (besides an Advertising Revenue Board) a Com-
munications Council which 'would have the right to demand
air time or column space for the correction of errors of
fact or redress of grievances.' It would make these demands
in the Government's name. It would be Government-
funded, it would be helping to prepare 'a national communi-
cations policy' for the Government, its members would be
Government-appointed. Its judgement of whether certain
selections of fact constituted 'errors of fact', or of what
counted as 'grievances', would be in danger of approximat-
ing to the Government's own; and journalists, unanxious
to expend space on corrections, would be tempted to trim
in the direction they thought the Council would approve.

The TUC, in its evidence to the McGregor Commission,
suggested a National Press Finance Corporation which
would own and run presses, leasing them to such newspapers as it chose. The NUJ backed a similar scheme.
NATSOPA wanted such a body to own and run a number
of newspapers as well. NALGO (the National and Local

121

Government Officers' Association) would have extended the same favour to all newspapers and their means of distribution, with an Independent Press Authority to license them. These proposals had no immediate prospect of coming to birth. But it was not unthinkable that a future Labour Government would enact a version of them; and they came a little nearer with the McGregor Commission's interim proposal during 1976 for Government help with modernization loans.

Such schemes addressed the problem of the wasteful use of printing presses and of printing manpower, and the high cost of starting a new newspaper. They did not deal with the intractable truth that, wherever it finds patronage, a newspaper must in the end find a good supply of readers if it is to survive. More than that, they ignored the point that newspapers which accept help from the State, in money or kind, are inhibited from keeping the cool watch on the State's performance which is among their main obligations.

For all that, it would be wrong to represent journalism and Government as adversaries and nothing else. At the least they are adversaries who depend on one another, like professional wrestlers endlessly renewing the same bout in different rings. Government needs journalists in order to have its deeds and expectations publicly set out. Journalism, anxious to make the world as interesting and comprehensible as possible, constantly asks the Government machine for help – information from the ministry press office, an interview with the minister himself. Government may want to divert journalism into different preoccupations, but the mutual dependence is there. The point is valid for journalists of the written as well as the spoken word; but it is especially true of broadcasters. An indispensable element in broadcast journalism is the body in the studio. If events face a minister with a sudden challenge, newspapermen can if necessary piece his attitudes together from other sources; television or radio journalists have an evident hole in their coverage if they cannot broadcast an interview with him. Harold

Wilson, perfectly understanding these things, and finding certain BBC men lacking in the deference due to a Prime Minister, would sometimes punish the BBC by refusing it an interview and giving one exclusively to a journalist from ITV.

The clearest expression of the interdependence of journalism and Government is the group of parliamentary journalists (newspapermen and broadcasters, to the number of about eighty) known as the Lobby. They are so called because they are licensed by the Commons Serjeant-at-Arms (on the nomination of their own employers) to stand about in the Members' Lobby and accost the stray backbencher. But they spend comparatively little time doing that. Their principal source is the Government. They have a room of their own at the Commons, up a winding stair and overlooking the river; and there they often gather to listen to ministers who have a new Bill to explain or an embarrassment to smooth away. On Thursday afternoons, after the statement in the Chamber of the business for the following week, they hear in succession from the Leader of the House and the Leader of the Opposition. Besides that they have individual dealings with other politicians on the front benches and the back, and with Whitehall press officers; and they are allowed an early dip in the broad stream of Government White Papers and Green Papers and Bills and announcements and reports.

They also have regular meetings, sometimes twice daily, with the Prime Minister's press staff. Although that arrangement was closed down in June 1975 by Harold Wilson's Press Secretary, Joe Haines, the encounters were resumed as soon as James Callaghan took over as Prime Minister in April 1976. They were too useful to both sides to do without.

The value of all these encounters, to politicians and journalists, was that notionally they had not even happened. Although it was occasionally breached, the general practice was that politicians did not mention any such meeting, and journalists used the information given them without attributing it to a named source. Haines, in his letter to the Lobby's chairman, gave it as his own and Wilson's opinion that the custom was good neither for the Government nor for the press nor above all for the general public.

> I think many people rightly suspect the validity of stories which lean heavily upon thin air. From now on, it will be my general rule that if a statement needs to be made on behalf of the Prime Minister, that statement will be made on the record.
>
> This will not lead to any loss of information to the general public. Indeed, they will then know its source. And it will eliminate the kind of extreme absurdity where, under the rules governing the present meetings, even the name of the annual Poppy Day seller who calls on the Prime Minister is given unattributably.

Yet in fact it was exactly that anonymity which made the custom so serviceable. Politicians could get the exposure they needed for their views without the embarrassment of being held to every word of them. They could promise action without needing to be specific about detail. They could establish what might be the public reaction to a certain line of policy without ever openly mooting it. Busy journalists, for their part, had the freedom either to dignify their sources – to transmute a press officer or a Parliamentary Private Secretary into 'senior ministers' – or to mention none at all. It was a practice which extended beyond Westminster to the groups of specialist correspondents clustering round particular departments of State – Education, for example, or the Environment. The interests of politician and journalist were not identical; yet both were served by a system of frequent and unpublicized contacts.

There are points where the two interests meet; and for journalists those are the most difficult areas of all. Journalists are also citizens. As such they are no more adversaries of Government than the great body of the citizenry is.

They want the country to be well run, to overcome its problems at home and abroad. In so far as those are tasks for Government, they want the Government to succeed.

In most areas of life, that sets up no conflict. Ordinary reporting of what the Government is doing ought to help it: its aims will then be understood and shared. To report facts which suggest that the policy is misconceived or badly executed or unsuccessful, or to carry critical comment by people outside Government, or to voice criticisms editorially, may be just as helpful: it may set the Government on a wiser course than before.

The difficulty arises when those unfavourable observations themselves become facts in the case. To observe something, if the observation is known, is often to change it. To declare that a certain Government enterprise is failing may hasten its failure: people may cease to take it seriously, or may intensify their efforts to overthrow it. In such instances the journalist may be acting directly contrary to his fellow citizens' best interests – and to his own as a citizen. The problem becomes acute when the issue is the national economy or a national war effort.

Economic journalists report and discuss the state of the economy as gauged from all kinds of indices; and their words are relayed abroad. If they stress strikes, then the foreign buyer will be wary of British exports, in case they are not delivered on time. If they suggest – a particularly sensitive matter, this – that the pound sterling is overvalued, then the opinion may come true merely by being uttered: foreign businessmen will delay buying the sterling they need for purchases in Britain, in the expectation that the price will go down; British businessmen – newspaper managements buying Canadian or Finnish newsprint, for example – will buy the necessary foreign currency as early as they can; and this process of eager selling and tardy buying will depress sterling further, with a consequent ill effect on prices in British shops.

If that were the whole of the argument, there would be a

strong obligation on journalists to put as favourable a construction on economic events as they could. But it would be impossible to decide which strikes were forces for good, and single out only those for attention; and suggesting that factories were very seldom stopped in Britain would induce a complacency about industrial relations which would in the long term be even more damaging than foreign scorn. With sterling, equally, journalistic reticence can be more harmful than frankness. Sterling was over-valued for three years after Harold Wilson first took office as Prime Minister – from October 1964 until November 1967. Wilson ruled out not just devaluation but any discussion of it in Whitehall. Economic journalists largely felt it their duty to fall in with that. For three years, in order to defend the sterling parity, Wilson had to flout his Government's social aims by cutting Government spending (to show foreign sterling-holders that Britain's books were being properly balanced). When the inevitable devaluation finally came, it was too late to take advantage of the fading boom in world trade. Journalists might have shown the higher patriotism if they had spoken up.

War engages a whole nation's interests even more squarely than commerce, and depends in much the same way on confidence. If journalists report that their country's operations are being ineptly conducted, it has a doubly damaging effect: it lessens their own side's willingness to prosecute the war, and increases the enemy's. With that in mind, a great many war correspondents during the past hundred years have put their duty to their country in front of their duty to truth. A notable example was the corps of British war correspondents on the Western Front in the First World War. They saw what their conducting officers allowed them to see, and sent what army censors allowed them to send.

In consequence their reports of the war emerged as detached and cheerful. They revealed nothing of the infinite misery of trench warfare, nothing of the incompetence and callousness among British generals, nothing of the unimaginable scale of the slaughter. The correspondents could not altogether know how much they were failing to report; but to the extent that they did know, they and their employers at home (who might have changed the system by a concerted stand) acquiesced in the failure because of what seemed the paramount importance of keeping up recruiting. Again, it was a duty misread. If the press had told the truth, people at home urging an end to the war would have been better furnished with fact.

Any settlement of the dilemma is painful. Just over half a century later, Northern Ireland brought the problem even nearer home. In July 1970, British troops were taken on in guerrilla warfare there by a breakaway group of the Irish Republican Army – the Provisionals. It was a civil conflict, and there was no censorship: none would have been possible while the facts could be freely reported in the Irish Republic. National self-confidence was at a low ebb. British journalism felt able to regard British troops with a cold eye. It reported their occasional acts of cruelty and their constant ill-success. It gave space, and even praise, to the war aim of the men they were fighting – which was in essence that British military and political influence should be withdrawn from Northern Ireland. The effect was to encourage Provisionals in the belief that their cause was right, and to bring British withdrawal nearer, with uncertain consequences.

Journalists who took that course could justify it, as citizens, by the argument that the war effort was doing Britain harm and could do Ireland no good: although the British had (as the colonizing power) begun the Irish conflict, they had long lost the power to settle it. The fact remained that the Provisionals were a misguided body of men whose understanding of history was as weak as their moral sense, and their military defeat would have been a perfectly satisfactory outcome – if it could have been attained. In their work, journalists did not have to choose between different ends if they did not want to: they simply reported things as they found them. As citizens, though, they had to face the fact that their work sometimes made one outcome a little likelier than another.

For a journalist, there is a tension between the claims of his country and the claims of his work. It cannot be shrugged off with a word about allegiance owed only to humanity at large. A journalist is a member of the State he lives in, like it or not, and he accepts the obligations with the benefits of membership. The tension can never be entirely resolved.

Chapter 8: The Law

Because the journalist is also a citizen, he is at a special disadvantage in his intermittent struggle with the State. The State makes the laws. In a parliamentary democracy they are in origin an expression of public opinion, the collective wisdom of most of the electorate. They are in general, for journalists as for everybody else, a useful guide and guard; but they sometimes restrict journalistic enterprise harmfully.

Public opinion by itself is seldom an active drag. At its simplest, it makes its weight felt in newspaper sales and broadcast ratings. These are vague clues, though: they give no precise picture of what is approved or disapproved, nor by whom. So they are easily neglected. A large body of readers and listeners and viewers then finds its opinion flouted, and feels a grievance against journalists even while it continues to absorb their product. Aggrieved in their turn, journalists cast about for an antidote.

The first one they find is a code of conduct. The NUJ has had one in the back of its rule book since 1936. Many newspapers operate them, more or less consciously. Few reporters, for example, would now allow themselves the tactic which was once standard for visits to a dramatically bereaved household – to steal a photograph of the dead off the mantelpiece. Journalists believe that they are quite well enough in touch with public opinion to draw up a code which will set minds at rest; and the device has the great advantage that it imposes no constraint from outside.

But it is as difficult to codify right conduct for journalists as for anybody else. You can equip yourself with the principle of avoiding methods of investigation which you would not want disclosed, and of giving people a chance to correct mistakes about themselves, and of weighing the importance of a story against its effect on people's lives; and when you come to apply your principles to a given situation, you can still find yourself in disagreement with your colleagues or competitors. The upshot is that a code makes very little difference either to conduct or to public hostility.

The next step is to find code-interpreters – people who are aware of these presumed principles as representatives of the public and can read them off against instances of disputed journalistic behaviour. This is to institutionalize public opinion; and there has been a lot of it. The BBC's Board of Governors, the members of the Independent Broadcasting Authority and their train of advisory bodies all represent attempts to bring lay judgement to bear on the practice of broadcasting. The complaints review bodies set up in 1971 were manned by laymen. Lay influence within the Press Council, too, has increased steadily. After the 1964 changes the Council still drew only a fifth of its members from outside journalism, and chose them itself. In July 1972 the Younger Committee on Privacy (besides suggesting changes in the review bodies' procedure) recommended that half the Council should be non-journalists, and that an independent appointments commission should choose them. The second recommendation was carried out in April 1973; and in July lay representation was increased to a third on the full Council, and half on the Council's complaints committee.

But these complaints bodies, including the Press Council, fell a long way short of the might of the law. Indeed, they were a substitute for it. They all demanded of the complainant that (at least in cases where an action at law might lie) he should sign an undertaking not to take the same complaint to law. The contention was that otherwise he would be unfairly helped in the subsequent legal action by knowing the defence which the newspaper or broadcasting organization had offered to the original complaint. So the only consequence which journalism had to fear from a complaint to these bodies was the making public of an unfavourable finding.

They did not even possess (or did not wish to exercise)

the freedom to conduct general examinations of journalistic performance – how fairly industrial news was reported, for example. That was left to dons. In the 1960s the character of journalists, and the nature and effect of their work, became a favourite subject for academic study. Compared with the classics of literature, the raw material was dispiriting, but it was at least plentiful and constantly renewed. If well done, the work could confront journalists with their failings and shame them into improvement. But that was all. None of these efforts at bringing public opinion to bear on journalism could significantly inhibit its liberty.

Where public opinion has crystallized into law, on the other hand, inhibitions abound. The argument for a free press is that it confers freedom on the voters: it furnishes them with the evidence they need on which to choose and maintain as sound a Government as possible. They do not need a press which is free to say what it likes without any possible ill consequences to itself. If it was, it could pre-judge trials, broadcast the secrets of the State's defences, ruin lives with lies. What is required is that the rightness or wrongness of the press's publishing a certain thing should not be judged before publication. If the new fact or allegation is suppressed in advance, then the voters cannot tell whether they would have been the better for knowing it or not. Sir William Blackstone, the eighteenth-century jurist, delivered in his *Commentaries* (16th edn, p. 151) an opinion still used in the courts:

> The liberty of the press is indeed essential to the nature of a free State; but this consists in laying no previous restraints upon publication, and not in freedom from censure for criminal matter when published.

On the face of it, English law and practice make little attempt to lay 'previous restraints' on publication. Yet a problem arises where the law is uncertain: it makes journalists draw back in doubt. The law at issue is partly case law, built up out of precedents, and partly statute law.

One of the oldest rights which journalists must take account of is parliamentary privilege. (Nearly all breaches of it are technically contempts of the House of Commons.) The notion goes back to the early fifteenth century: it arises from the belief that if elected members of a sovereign Parliament are to work efficiently they need certain immunities. For journalists, this has come to mean that two kinds of publication in particular are discouraged: any matter which diminishes public respect for the House, and any premature report of the doings of Commons committees.

The rule about respect is untroublesome. It has chiefly been used by MPs to protest against the occasional journalistic suggestion that some of their number accept inducements they ought not, or drink too much, or even snore during all-night sittings. Solemn deliberation on this sort of stuff by senior MPs banded into a Committee of Privileges has a way of making the House a good deal more ridiculous than the original charge did; and far more instances are let go than are pursued. Nor are the penalties crushing. Nominally they have always included imprisonment; and until the mid-nineteenth century it was regularly used. But since then it has come to seem disproportionate, and the fiercest punishment meted out has been a reprimand at the Bar of the House – something which a late-twentieth-century editor would wear like a campaign ribbon.

The ban on reporting committee proceedings before the due date of publication is in principle a little more awkward. It is a survival from the period (brought to an end by the successful protests of the politician-journalist John Wilkes in 1771) when all parliamentary business was secret, on the theory that openness inhibited frank speaking. In October 1975 a Commons committee was examining the idea of a wealth tax. The *Economist* published details from a draft report which the committee was still hesitating over. The Committee of Privileges was wheeled into action. It found the *Economist* article 'damaging to the work of Parliament' (*First Report from the Committee of Privileges, Session 1975–6*, November 1975, par. 3). It recommended that the editor and the article's author shou both be 'excluded from the precincts of the House for six months', and that the House should empower itself to impose fines in such cases in the future – in line with a suggestion made when the whole question had last been examined (*Report from the Select Committee on Parliamentary Privilege*, December 1967, par. 195).

If parliamentary committees became a forum for national discussion, and if heavy fines were indeed added to the penalties for publicizing them, then there might well be a loss in public knowledge and participation. But the Commons rejected its Privileges Committee's advice, the *Economist*'s men retained the freedom of the Palace of Westminster, and parliamentary committees in general remained peripheral to the national life. In so far as parliamentary privilege continued to be a check on editorial action, it was chiefly for the uncertainty about where and how heavily the stroke would fall.

More genuinely menacing to editors is the less exotic type of contempt – contempt of court. This, too, is not a matter of statute law: it is what judges have said it is. For journalists, it is contempt of court to publish anything which interferes with a fair trial by putting ideas of guilt or innocence into the minds of judge or jury. The penalties can be real. In 1949 an editor of the *Daily Mirror* was sent to prison for three months, and his company fined £10,000, for publishing a story about a man charged with murder which said that he was a human vampire and had committed other murders. In October 1967 Times Newspapers were fined £5000 because the *Sunday Times* had described a man as 'brothel-keeper, procurer and property racketeer': he turned out to be awaiting trial at Reading.

No sensible journalist would deny that those were offences against justice which deserved deterrent punishment.

The awkwardness, once again, is in the uncertainty. The accepted doctrine is that nothing prejudicial should be published when a trial is imminent. But how close must it be to count as imminent? The fact that suits were pending stifled serious journalistic comment on the thalidomide disaster for ten years. It was partly this case which prompted the setting up in June 1971 of a committee under Lord Justice Phillimore to see whether the law needed changing.

The committee reported (cmnd 5749) in December 1974; and it recommended that the question of imminence should be cleared up. It urged that the possibility of contempt should arise in criminal cases only after a charge had been made, and in civil cases only when a case had been set down for trial (though dissentient opinion on the committee and among judges thought that a little late). Had that recommendation been law in 1961, there would have been no risk in journalistic comment on the slow pace of the thalidomide settlements; and the Attorney-General's 1966 threat of contempt actions before the Aberfan tribunal would have been vain.

The other fault commonly found with the law of contempt as it stood was that it admitted no defence of public benefit. A series of connected frauds around the country, for example, could not be revealed for what it was while a single related case was awaiting trial. The public would remain unwarned. Phillimore and his colleagues decided against a public-benefit defence; but they did recommend that contempt should be in question only if a publication risked seriously impeding or prejudicing the course of justice, and that (par. 216 (15)):

It should be a defence to an allegation of contempt to show that a publication formed part of a legitimate discussion of matters of general public interest and that it only incidentally and unintentionally created a risk of serious prejudice to particular proceedings.

Those counts, too, would have been a help in the thalidomide affair.

That case showed up another legal obstacle for journalists: the law of confidence. The long article about the drug's marketing which the *Sunday Times* finally published in June 1976, once the contempt injunction had been lifted, did not even then contain all the relevant detail the paper knew. Part of it was company memoranda from Distillers (whose subsidiary made the drug, and who always denied negligence). In July 1974 Distillers had won an injunction in the High Court to stop the paper publishing these, on the ground that they were the company's copyright, and that to report them even indirectly would be a breach of confidence.

The body of case law which makes up the law of confidence is based on two cases: one is about the unauthorized publication of a collection of etchings of Prince Albert's, the other about the disclosure of a secret recipe for an unpatented medicine. The law is concerned with private interest, therefore, not public. Newspaper lawyers have argued that, here too, a public-interest defence ought to be admissible.

They made the same point about any law that might be enacted to protect privacy. In a free country, people expect not to be intruded on and not to have their affairs known except by their own wish. Of late years these expectations have been more often disappointed than they used to be. Part of the reason is that a welfare state needs to know a good deal about its citizens (though Governments have never acknowledged that as a cause for concern). Part is technical advance: computers centralize private information (particularly financial and academic records) which outsiders can sometimes tap, and special lenses and microphones of great sensitivity make unofficial spying easy. In the late 1960s these developments prompted a number of backbench attempts at legislation to establish a right of privacy. Although they failed, the setting up of the Committee on Privacy under Sir Kenneth Younger (a former Labour minister) in May 1970 was a direct consequence, and when the Committee's report (cmnd 5012) was published in July 1972 it urged certain new rules about acquiring and handling private information. But scientific advances were not the only source of anxiety. It also derived from the behaviour of journalists.

Newspapermen had regularly offended against privacy. They had pushed in where they were not welcome, and they had published information about people who wanted it kept secret. They argued that this intrusiveness was in the public interest, as when a firm was suspected of fraud; but they sometimes fostered a confusion between what was in the public interest and what was merely of interest to a curious public, as when a prominent figure's sexual habits were at issue. These ancient inclinations seemed intensified, during the 1960s, both by the spreading fashion for investigative journalism and by the growth in the number of broadcasting organizations. Their lights and cables and recording gear made them appear more physically intrusive, at the scene of a mining accident or outside a private house, than men with notebooks and still cameras ever had.

The Younger Committee gave more of its attention to journalistic intrusion than to any other kind. In the end it only recommended such changes in the Press Council and the broadcasting complaints bodies as might make them more sensitive to public representations. It argued against any new law providing a general right of privacy: it perceived the unavoidable conflict with 'the right to speak and publish the truth', and concluded (par. 43) that things were best left as they were:

> On balance we have come to be more impressed with the risks involved in propounding a rather general law, the scope of whose impact upon other important rights seems uncertain, than we are either with the seriousness of the residual wrongs which might thereby be righted or the effectiveness of the legal remedy proposed.

But the possibility of legislation remained, and journalists knew that they might at any time be called on both to justify their principle and to improve their practice.

The brand of privacy which chiefly interests politicians in Government is the privacy of governmental discussion and decision – the whole area of official secrets. The question had been raised by a series of disputes: the D notice affair in February 1967, the *Sunday Telegraph* case in January 1970, the *Railway Gazette* raid in November 1972, the publishing of the Crossman diaries from January 1975 on, the leak of Cabinet papers to *New Society* in June 1976. It was these last two cases which tipped the Callaghan Government over into an intention to legislate; and agreement within the Cabinet was made easier by Roy Jenkins's leaving it.

Jenkins, responsible for the Official Secrets Act as Home Secretary for the second time after the February 1974 election, believed it to be far too sweeping. In his Granada Guildhall lecture in March 1975 (*Government, Broadcasting and the Press* – Hart-Davis, MacGibbon) he asked:

Why ... do we need our tight, restrictive, hastily passed even if infrequently used Official Secrets Act to protect our relatively minor post-imperial role? The simple answer is that we don't and that the most controversial part of it, section 2, should and will be repealed and replaced by far less wide-ranging and severe safeguards against the unauthorized disclosure of information. The criminal law, I think, need be involved very little. Professional civil service discipline should be enough to deal with nearly all practical difficulties.

But in September 1976 Jenkins left the Cabinet to prepare for his new work as President of the European Commission in Brussels. Sterner-minded ministers were free to follow their inclination. They had had a blueprint for reform available for four years, since the Franks Committee had reported in 1972. Its brief had been only 'to review the operation of section 2 of the Official Secrets Act 1911 and to make recommendations'. It therefore made no suggestions about the D notice system – which in truth editors found mildly embarrassing, since it implied their voluntary co-operation in censorship, but not oppressive, since it was very little used. The Franks report addressed itself to that part of the law which had been specifically discredited by the failure of the case against the *Sunday Telegraph*; and it concluded (cmnd 5104, par. 276):

Section 2 of the Official Secrets Act 1911 should be repealed, and replaced by a new statute, called the Official Information Act, which should apply only to official information which –

a. is classified information relating to defence or internal security, or to foreign relations, or to the currency or to the reserves, the unauthorized disclosure of which would cause serious injury to the interests of the nation; *or*

b. is likely to assist criminal activities or to impede law enforcement; *or*

c. is a Cabinet document; *or*

d. has been entrusted to the Government by a private individual or concern.

It would be an offence, under these proposals, for anyone entrusted with such information to pass it on without leave, or for anyone at all to use it if there were grounds for believing it had been unlawfully come by, or to use it for private gain. 'The mere receipt of official information', though, 'should no longer be an offence.' Information was to count as 'classified' if it was marked SECRET, or if it related to military weapons or equipment and was marked DEFENCE – CONFIDENTIAL. Ultimate arbiter of a document's grading was to be the departmental minister concerned.

Roy Jenkins's successor at the Home Office was Merlyn

Rees – who as an Opposition MP had himself been a member of the Franks Committee. He was also a long-standing political associate of the Prime Minister's. In a parliamentary statement (*Commons Hansard*, 22 November 1976) he announced that the Government had concluded that section 2 of the 1911 Act 'should be replaced by an Official Information Act on the broad lines recommended by the Franks Committee', though legislation could not be introduced for at least a year. But it would not be Franks plain:

> In security and intelligence, defence and international relations, the Government have concluded that some rearrangement and extension of the Franks categories is required. Information relating to security and intelligence matters is deserving of the highest protection whether or not it is classified. The Government propose therefore that this should form a separate category.
>
> In the defence field the Franks Committee recommended that confidential information relating to military weapons and equipment should be given the special marking of DEFENCE – CONFIDENTIAL and be protected by criminal sanctions.
>
> The Government have concluded that confidential information of a sensitive and potentially damaging kind goes rather wider than this in both the defence and international fields. It extends to certain areas of defence policy and strategy and of international relations where unauthorized disclosure would be prejudicial to British interests, to relations with a foreign Government or to the safety of British citizens.
>
> The Government therefore propose to extend this Franks concept to become DEFENCE AND INTERNATIONAL – CONFIDENTIAL and to define it somewhat more widely than Franks.

The Rees statement nevertheless claimed that this represented 'a system more liberal than that proposed by the Franks

Committee'. The claim was based on the decision to exclude two kinds of material from the proposed law's range. One was information about the currency and the reserves, which had become less sensitive with the end (since Franks reported) of fixed exchange rates. The other was Cabinet and Cabinet committee documents. They dealt mainly with domestic affairs, the statement said, and their protection was basically a matter of 'trust and good sense among colleagues'.

Taken earlier, that decision would have saved Special Branch time over the *Railway Gazette* case, and a certain amount of fruitless sleuthing over the retailing of Cabinet minutes in *New Society*. When that article appeared, the head of the Civil Service (Sir Douglas Allen) was set on to discover its source. At the end of a fortnight's work he had found nothing. The Prime Minister then told the Commons, early in July 1976, that there would be no prosecution under the Official Secrets Act either of the article's author (Frank Field) or of anyone concerned in its publication. But a police search for guilty civil servants went on; and a new inquiry was set up, under Lord Houghton (a former member of Wilson Cabinets), into the rules about Cabinet documents generally. The report of the three-man Houghton Committee (cmnd 6677) was published at the end of November, a week after the Rees statement. It adopted a Cabinet Office suggestion that each department should have a 'Cabinet Documents Officer' who would have 'overall responsibility for the arrangements for the receipt, distribution and custody of all Cabinet and Cabinet committee documents'. The Prime Minister told the Commons that the Government once again 'broadly accepted' the recommendations, and was considering their detailed application.

The nature of Governments, and ministers, had not much changed. There were serious arguments from efficiency for keeping Cabinet proceedings secret; but there were even more pressing arguments from embarrassment.

Ministers had lately been reminded of that by publication in the *Sunday Times* during October and November 1976 of extracts from the second volume of the Crossman diaries. They covered the first half of the second Wilson Government, between 1966 and 1968; and they gave a strong impression of ministers preoccupied with the trivia of personal status – Crossman not least – in the midst of overwhelming events. (James Callaghan had himself been Chancellor of the Exchequer until the enforced devaluation of sterling in November 1967.)

Yet ministers need not have worried. The Crossman phenomenon would continue to be rare. That followed chiefly from the fact that not one Cabinet minister in a hundred commands the journalistic gifts he did – the eye for the telling detail, the skill to catch it in words. But besides that the restraints of both law and custom had been screwed a little tighter than before.

The law about Cabinet confidences stood where Lord Widgery, the Lord Chief Justice, had left it. He gave judgement in the High Court in October 1975 in the case in which the Attorney-General, Sam Silkin, for the Government, had tried to stop publication of the first Crossman volume in book form. Widgery's central finding was that the doctrine of confidence did extend beyond commercial and domestic to political secrets, and that a Cabinet minister could be restrained by law from 'improper publication' of information confidentially received. It is true that Widgery then surprised the court by letting the book through, on the ground that the events described in it – being 'up to ten years old' – were too far in the past for the principle of Cabinet confidentiality to suffer harm. But he did not say what period of time was enough; nor, more important, did he explain which kinds of material of the many in the diaries broke the law of confidence. Intending ministerial diarists were left to conclude that the only safe way to stay out of trouble with the law was not to keep a diary at all.

To the new interpretation of the law was added a new

rule of custom. In April 1975, between the ending of the serialization of the first volume in the *Sunday Times* and the Government's attempt in the courts to stop the book itself, Harold Wilson had set up a committee on ministerial memoirs. Its chairman was Lord Radcliffe, a former Lord of Appeal, and among the other six members was again Lord Franks. The committee's report (cmnd 6386) was published in January 1976. It found against new legislation, thus leaving the field to the Widgery judgement of three months before. It resanctified the convention (which until the Crossman case had been growing firmer since the 1920s) that ministerial memoirs should be vetted by the Secretary to the Cabinet. For confidential matter it set a quarantine period of fifteen years. That looked for a moment like a generous compromise between Widgery and the Public Records Act 1967, which stipulated a lag of thirty years. But the Act covered official records (which are notoriously laconic about Cabinet meetings), not ministers' own recollections. Radcliffe was proposing a new embargo.

It was adopted at once. Wilson announced (*Commons Hansard*, 22 January 1976) that his Government accepted the Radcliffe report in full, and that he would be inviting 'all present ministers . . . to sign an appropriate declaration'. There were refusals; some senior ministers already had contracts with newspapers or publishers; and the matter was not pressed. But the fifteen-year rule was there as the expected standard. Ministers would clearly be no more help than before as detailed journalistic sources.

Besides Phillimore on contempt, Younger on privacy and Franks on secrecy, the Government had had in front of it since March 1975 a fourth report about the law of journalism: Faulks on defamation. It reviewed the working of statute and case law about libel and its spoken equivalent, slander. The committee chairman was Sir Neville Faulks, a High Court judge, who as a barrister had specialized in libel cases.

The possibility of a libel suit is undoubtedly a risk which

newspaper lawyers keep in the front of their minds. It occasions a good deal of guarded writing, sometimes to the public's short-term detriment. If an insurance company is on the point of collapse, there would be virtue in reporting the fact, so as to stop people at large from taking out policies which will soon be worthless; but newspapers do not do it, since the report itself might hasten the collapse or dissuade rescue, and the company might be able to collect compensatory damages for libel. Few journalists, on the other hand, and even fewer people outside journalism, would be happy if damaging statements could be published on mere suspicion. Both fairness and accuracy are in general served by a system which forbids damaging statements unless they are provably true, and allows them as long as they are.

The Faulks report (cmnd 5909) recommended no essential change in that pattern. Truth should remain a defence to a civil action for defamation. But a great many minor changes were proposed, to clarify the law. Among them was the combining of libel and slander into a single offence of defamation (which some editors feared might inhibit journalists from putting tough questions).

Both plaintiffs and defendants (who are commonly newspapers) have found that the chief practical difficulty about libel actions is the cost. They are expensive to bring, and can be very expensive to lose: in 1961 a jury awarded £100,000 against the *Daily Telegraph* and £117,000 against the *Daily Mail* because of the implications of a factual story about investigations by the Fraud Squad (though the Court of Appeal later ordered a new trial, and the matter was settled out of court). Faulks met both points by suggesting an extension of legal aid for libel cases, and an end to the jury's power to set the amount of damages.

The ancient offence called obscene libel was partially redefined in the Obscene Publications Act 1959. The Act was put on to the statute book by Roy Jenkins while he was an Opposition backbencher, chiefly to protect more-or-less serious works like Vladimir Nabokov's *Lolita* from

143

prosecution. His Act called in aid the concept of 'the public good'. This was taken up by the publishers of pornographic magazines: prosecuted under the Act, they regularly marshalled medical witnesses who claimed that pornography served the public good by releasing sexual tensions. A string of acquittals was brought to an end in November 1976 when the Law Lords upheld other judges in disallowing that defence, and the law on obscenity returned to its ordinary uncertainty.

It was not in any case a law which was likely to give journalists much trouble. Nor were two other paper tigers, the Race Relations Act 1976 (which came into force in June 1977) and the Rehabilitation of Offenders Act 1974. Common sense stood in the way. The new Race Relations Act made it an offence to publish threatening, abusive or insulting language in circumstances likely to stir up racial hatred. An intention to stir it up no longer needed proving. In principle, that could apply to the journalistic publication of racialist speeches made outside Parliament. In practice journalists were likely to go on ignoring such speeches, as they had for years, except where the source was undeniably significant; and if the Attorney-General nevertheless thought the public interest served by a prosecution in such cases, he would find it very difficult to show the necessary link between what was published and an actual manifestation of hatred.

The Rehabilitation of Offenders Act was an odd little piece of legislation designed to express society's forgiveness of people who had been duly punished. Once a specified length of time had elapsed after certain kinds of short prison terms, they became as though they had never been, and a newspaper or broadcasting organization which mentioned them might find itself sued for libel. But such suits were difficult to bring, and the Act was flouted by a number of newspapers in the month it came into force, July 1975. They reported a past conviction of a man involved in the attempt to force a Cabinet minister, Reg Prentice, out of his east London seat. Writs were brandished, but nothing happened.

In sum, the legal climate in which journalists work is a constantly changing one. The chief inhibitor of press freedom in the United Kingdom is the law. But the law is not carved on tables of stone. It varies with the changes made in it by Parliament, the successive interpretations of it put forward by judges, and the use made of it by litigants (including Government); and all those variations are a distant expression of public opinion. At any time, therefore, journalists are in a state of some uncertainty about what the law is, and different editors treat it with different degrees of robustness. In the mid-1970s that uncertainty was increased by the existence of four weighty reports to the Government about aspects of press law, and the Government's slowness in deciding what to do about them.

At one time ministers appeared to have decided on a sweet-and-sour bundle. Harold Wilson told the Liverpool Press Club (*The Times*, 6 March 1976) that 'In the Government's view changes in the laws on contempt and defamation . . . must be balanced by voluntary measures, agreed with the press, to guarantee the individual citizen and his family an effective right of privacy'; in other words, if we give you Phillimore and Faulks, you must accept Younger as well. But Wilson had already decided to resign his office; and when he went, a month later, he took his intentions with him. The only report in which the Callaghan Government showed any legislative interest was the other member of the quartet, Franks on secrecy. Clearly journalists could not expect relief in their legal perplexities from Government; and, given the long animosity between the two, there was no reason why they should.

PART THREE

*Policy alternatives
and likely developments*

Chapter 9: The Future

Since the Second World War, then, despite a good deal of arguing, the balance of forces within journalism has not been much altered. The number of national newspapers has gone on falling; but it has fallen no faster than it did in the period between the world wars, and the fact of there being fewer proprietors has not meant that fewer different voices have been heard, since proprietorial influence has been lessened by the developing self-confidence of journalists. In broadcasting, on the other hand, ownership has been hugely widened by the coming of commercial television and radio; and yet variety of outlook and output has not been comparably increased, both because of broadcasting's need to show political tact and because of the homogenizing effects of competition. Departures from standard patterns of thought and programming have been easier to find in the BBC's own lesser services than in those areas where it has had commercial competitors.

Advertising has continued to grow in importance as a source of newspaper revenue; but the only serious effect of that growth has been to intensify for newspapers the consequences of the recession which since 1967 the whole country has suffered. The unions, in this same postwar span of time, have shed the burden of national newspaper ownership and hardly begun to consider resuming it. As a means towards influencing the content of journalism they have preferred to rely on their traditional instrument, industrial action; and yet the proportion of instances where they have used it to that end has been minute.

The relation between journalism and the State has not changed significantly. The State's power over newspapers remains small, over broadcasting large – and largely unused (though the formal ban on broadcast editorializing is observed, and is a limitation). Journalism and government remain dependent on one another: journalists for information, governors for the publicizing of their concerns. (One useful consequence of a row about nepotism in May 1977 was to lay the chief mechanism in that interdependence open to the public gaze. James Callaghan sanctioned the posting of his son-in-law, Peter Jay, to Washington as British ambassador; and he then allowed his Press Secretary, Tom McCaffrey, to defend the appointment by implying to the Lobby that the superseded ambassador was unsuitable anyway. Lobby journalists, as convention dictated, published the judgement without saying in so many words where it came from; Conservative MPs nevertheless perceived the source and exclaimed against unfair use of a covert channel; and the resulting dispute obliged newspapers to explain on their front pages the system of Downing Street briefings which both briefers and briefed had till then pretended to be non-existent.)

A greater inhibitor of press freedom than the State, during these years, has been the law; and the inhibition follows more from uncertainty than from any actual oppressiveness, either in drafting or application.

The strongest influence has undoubtedly remained the reader, the listener, the viewer. The reader, in particular, has again and again been shown to wield more power over the content and survival of newspapers than proceeds from any other single quarter. Listeners and viewers are less directly influential: broadcasting organizations are set up and cast down by agencies of the State, and since listeners and viewers pay less directly for what they get than the reader, they show their approval or disapproval less clearly. But audience sizes are carefully computed, and nothing else is so important in determining a programme's place in the schedules. Besides that, one perceptible postwar change has been the establishment of bodies designed to register the individual citizen's complaints about what he reads or hears or sees, and if possible to satisfy them: the Press Council, the complaints boards devised by the BBC and the IBA. It is clear that such bodies have further to go yet.

The various forces contending to have the media run as they would like are thus in much the same relative positions as they have been for three decades at least. None is defeated, none dominant. Will that rough equipoise persist?

Two aids to prediction which came to hand during 1977 were the Annan report on broadcasting (published in March) and the McGregor report on the press (published in July). As guides to the future they could not be wholly reliable: many of their suggestions required action or inaction from the Government, and these are stimuli to which Governments have a long history of sluggish or perverse response. At the same time, the two previous pairs of postwar reports on the media had at least helped create the atmosphere in which broadcasting and the press continued to develop. If that happened again, the pace of change would not be headlong: the two reports were predominantly conservative in tone.

The Annan Committee had wrestled with many of the general problems which confronted the Beveridge Committee in the late 1940s and the Pilkington Committee in the early 1960s. Beveridge faced doubts about the sheer size of the BBC, and whether licence-fee revenue would go on sufficing it. So did Annan. Pilkington considered the edgy relation between Government and broadcasters, and the effect on the nation's moral and cultural life of the commercially-inspired chase after big audiences. So did Annan; and the recurrent question of whether existing broadcasters should have their franchises renewed was complicated, for Annan, by the need to recommend a use for the unused fourth television channel.

The findings (*Report of the Committee on the Future of Broadcasting*, cmnd 6753) largely upheld existing dispositions. Political arrangements should stay. 'On balance we conclude that, while some improvements could be made, the relations between Government and Parliament and the Broadcasting Authorities do not require much adjustment: the chain of accountability is adequate.' (Par 5.38.) The BBC should keep its four national radio services, its two television channels and its practice of drawing its income almost entirely from licence-fees. ITV, similarly, should retain its single channel, advertisement-financed, with slightly increased stress on its regional character.

The one mild jolt to the existing order was the proposal that both the BBC and the IBA should lose their local radio stations to a new Local Broadcasting Authority: it would encourage diversity of ownership and finance, though the main source of income would be advertising. As for the fourth television channel, that should go in due time to another new body, an Open Broadcasting Authority. It 'would operate more as a publisher of programme material provided by others' (7.11); it would carry educational programmes (including those for the Open University), programmes made by individual ITV companies and ITN, and offerings from independent producers; its sources of revenue would include advertisements (grouped into blocks), sponsoring, and educational grants; and it would be sent out from IBA transmitters.

The proposals were summed up in these terms (30.3–5):

In the 21 years since the opening of commercial broadcasting, the BBC and the IBA provided in competition a regulated duopoly. We believe that in future broadcasting services should be provided by establishing more Authorities in regulated diversity.

Regulated diversity means that each Broadcasting Authority is responsible for giving its own type of service. They should not provide exactly the same services nor should they compete for exactly the same source of finance. That is why we recommend that local broadcasting be put under a new Authority, and that the fourth channel for the whole of the United Kingdom should not be allotted to either the BBC or the IBA but to another new authority. We want the broadcasting industry to grow. But we do not want more of the same. There are enough programmes for the majority; and if new authorities too compete for vast audiences, the quality of service on the existing channels will decline. What is needed now is programmes for the different minorities which add up to make the majority. That is why we want to expand local radio, and eventually launch local television. That is why we want new ventures in educational broadcasting, above all for adults who need to retrain for new jobs to take up different careers. We want each service to be mixed, and we are opposed to, for instance, an educational channel, which would give only one type of service. That is why we want the fourth channel to be the host to different companies, different kinds of broadcasters, different kinds of programmes, some of which could not get on the air on any other channel.

In making our recommendations we have recognized that the changes we foresee or recommend cannot take place overnight. The nation's economy must improve before broadcasting can expand. But in the eighties we hope the tide will sweep in, and the structure of broadcasting must be malleable enough to provide the country with genuinely new services.

A handful of the Annan Committee's members wanted to push this 'concept of pluralism' further by splitting the BBC into two separate corporations, one for radio and one for television, as a means to easing the 'internal anxiety, frustration and bureaucratic restriction' which flowed from the BBC's great size (9.31–42). The majority turned the idea down, mainly on the ground that 'the size of the BBC helps to protect its independence' (9.51). BBC managers themselves believed that discontent followed at least as much from the end of the Corporation's half-century of expansion: transfer and promotion were no longer easily had.

The report was more innovative in treating of disquiet in the public at large. The unimpeachable basis of the Committee's thought was that broadcasting was obliged to reflect the diversity of the nation it served; that this might involve transmitting crudities of speech and behaviour, fictional and real, which many listeners and viewers would fear to be corruptive of national standards; and that whether or not that fear was well based, it existed, and must be met and if possible assuaged. To that end, the report enjoined on production staff a heightened respect for the codes compiled by broadcasting managements; but it also recommended new ways to make public opinion count.

There should be a single Broadcasting Complaints Commission, replacing the BBC's and the IBA's private bodies, empowered to award costs if a complaint were upheld, and asking no undertaking that the case would not also be taken to the courts. There should be a Public Enquiry Board for Broadcasting, its task to hold seven-yearly public audits of the way each broadcasting authority had met its responsibilities, and to conduct hearings on other specific issues (violence on television, for example, or the use of a fifth channel). Besides that, the broadcasting authorities should themselves hold occasional public hearings on the performance of the broadcasters under their charge, and particularly on the award of franchises. And production staff should be asked to discuss their work with groups of viewers and listeners.

The report made a great many other deserving points – against advertisements in children's programmes; in favour (hesitantly) of advertising by charities; against party political broadcasts on all television channels at once, except during general elections; in favour of joint audience research between the BBC and ITV, and of moves towards a common programme journal. But most of these were matters for the broadcasters. It was the questions of structure, finance and accountability which remained for decision by politicians.

Foretelling those decisions was made difficult by the political conjuncture. Since current licences to broadcast were to expire in July 1979, legislation to renew or replace them would risk coming too late if it were not presented during the year of parliamentary business ending in October 1978. But there was no assurance that the Callaghan Government, weakened through by-election defeats and sustained only conditionally by the Liberals, could stay in power till then. The new Bill might come from either main party.

If it came from Labour, it would be as little controversial as possible. The Government would have no votes and no political credit to spare on avoidable arguments. Something of this was communicated in a Commons debate on Annan two months after its publication. Merlyn Rees, minister in charge of broadcasting as Home Secretary, endorsed the report where it suggested leaving things alone and cast gentle doubt on it where it proposed change. Of the Local Broadcasting Authority, he stressed the large number of letters sent to him (which were mostly written, like a good many to the papers at the time, to defend the separateness of the BBC's local stations). Of the Open Broadcasting Authority, he said that a question mark hung over its financial viability, and that its renunciation of 'the traditional responsibilities of the broadcasting authorities' would carry risks. The minority notion of bisecting the BBC was not even considered. The idea of a Public Enquiry Board for Broadcasting fared scarcely better: Rees said of it (Commons Hansard, 23 May 1977, col. 1026):

> I can see the attraction in the idea of public hearings, but I must tell the House that I do not think we should be justified in creating a new organization unless we were satisfied that this was clearly the only effective way to meet a demonstrable need.

The only plans for change which the Home Secretary seemed to look on benignly were the proposals for a Broadcasting Complaints Commission, which he described as attractive.

William Whitelaw, leading for the Opposition in the same debate, indicated that if the Bill fell to the Conservatives to bring in, their line would be similar but harder. The BBC should certainly not be split: its international standing, as well as its independence, would suffer. There should be no Local Broadcasting Authority, and no Public Enquiry

155

Board, on grounds of bureaucracy and cost – whereas a
Complaints Commission was a 'very modest extension of
bureaucracy', Whitelaw trusted, and would be welcomed.
The Open Broadcasting Authority idea, original and
imaginative though it was, contained a fatal flaw (cols.
1035, 1037):

> Proposals for financing it simply do not stand up to
> examination. The paragraph on finance bears all the
> hallmarks of an almost desperate search for ideas . . .
> I believe that the proposed new authority would be
> extremely reliant on the IBA and the ITV companies for
> many of the necessary transmission and technical services.
> It would therefore seem sensible to start the other way
> round, by giving the fourth channel to the IBA and ITV
> companies, which can immediately provide the necessary
> equipment and skills, but on conditions that would meet
> the Committee's main purpose.

That last proviso was important. The Open Broadcasting
Authority was the most valuable idea in the Annan report.
Neither the Public Enquiry Board not the Local Broadcasting Authority, unenacted, would be a major loss. A
Complaints Commission (to take the Enquiry Board first)
held certain hazards of its own: since it would need to be a
statutory body if it were to wield the powers proposed for
it, and since its findings would be used in evidence at
franchise-renewal time, it would increase the caution of
broadcasters in their dealings with the State; but given its
existence, and the proposed public hearings by the broadcasting authorities, an Enquiry Board would have little
useful left to do. As for the Local Broadcasting Authority,
Annan was right that variety of programming was likelier to
blossom under a single canopy than when a dual system
obliged pairs of local stations to compete by copying one
another's programmes; but it was difficult (on the evidence
of existing emissions) to believe that a thousand flowers
were waiting to bloom in local radio anyway, however

they were tended. In national television, on the other hand, Annan's contention had proven force. If the fourth television channel became merely ITV-2, and thus a direct competitor of BBC-2, it would pull BBC-2 down into imitative competition as surely as ITV-1 had pulled down BBC-1; and the viewer would then effectively be left with two choices still – between programmes like ITV-1 and programmes like ITV-2. Only if the fourth channel were obligatorily different from BBC-2 would diversity be genuinely increased. That was the justification for the Annan suggestion of a fourth channel which should publish material from a wide spread of different sources; and that was why the Conservative interest in observing at least that part of the Committee's intentions, whatever compromise was finally arrived at, was one which deserved upholding.

The McGregor Commission, similarly, addressed the same problems as its forerunners, Ross and Shawcross: narrowing or randomly changing ownership, sour relations between press and Government. As things had been, they remained: indeed, cases in point still arose so regularly that it was hard for the Commission to keep up to date. In April 1977, when its report was nearly ready, assorted financiers began a struggle for part or the whole of the Beaverbrook empire – the *Express* papers and the *Evening Standard* – which ended three months later when the entire group passed to a shipping and property concern named Trafalgar House. (Its managing director, Victor Matthews, showed engaging unawareness of several changed realities when he declared that his editors would have complete freedom as long as they agreed with the policy he had laid down – 'Believe in Britain and look for the good things'.) In May the *Daily Mail* published, with heavy denunciation, a letter implying ministerial complicity in the paying of bribes overseas – 'slush money' – by the largely nationalized motor firm British Leyland; and the letter turned out to be forged.

The *Mail* matter was put direct into Professor McGregor's hands by James Callaghan, in the clear expectation that the Commission's report would gain in severity as a result. But the Commission did not alter its judgements; and McGregor himself neatly summarized them in a late interpolation which explained why not (*Royal Commission on the Press, Final Report,* cmnd 6810, addendum to Chapter 10, pars. 5–11). Certainly the *Mail* story exemplified an old fault in parts of the press – 'the basing of contentious opinion on inaccurate information'; but the question was whether partisanship was so strong that exceptional measures to correct it would be justified.

> Many people and organizations complained to us of bias against the left on the part of the press as a whole. We have no doubt that over most of this century, the press has treated the beliefs and activities of the Labour movement with hostility. Such evidence as we have indicates that today it may be less partisan than its left-wing critics believe. It is certainly the case that some newspapers of the right persistently seek for discreditable material which can be used to damage the reputation of Labour ministers or those connected with the Party or with trade unions. The 'slush money' story is a lamentable example. Nevertheless, it is not new evidence that the *Daily Mail* is a polemical and politically partisan newspaper, for it has been that for a long time.

McGregor then set out in short form the reasons why the Commission, like its predecessor bodies, had decided against all the proposed mechanisms for correcting such imbalance as there was.

> We reject the idea of a launch fund to help new newspapers because we are opposed to the element of Government involvement in the press which would arise over the allocation of such a fund and because we have seen no scheme which we consider likely to have the editorial and economic results intended by those who put it forward. Furthermore, we cannot accept either that the creation of more newspapers, whether partisan or not, would be

likely to lessen the irresponsible conduct which is indulged in by some existing partisan newspapers, or that it would quieten political dissatisfaction with the contents and behaviour of the press.

McGregor did express the report's hope that the Labour movement would back the trade union project for a comprehensive paper of the left; and he went on to consider whether the law should be strengthened.

We believe as a general principle that the press should not operate under a special regime of law but should so far as possible stand before the law in the same way as any other organization or citizen.

Whether it is done by law or by voluntary measures, the only ways in which newspapers can be restrained are either by a process of monitoring before publication or by the application of sanctions afterwards. We reject the idea of monitoring before publication as censorship and entirely inconsistent with the freedom of the press. And . . . we reject the idea of sanctions such as fines and suspension of journalists, as both difficult to devise and enforce, and potentially dangerous to the freedom of the press.

Our firm belief is that the press should be left free to be partisan and restrained as at present only by the law and by the voluntary system of a Press Council greatly strengthened in the ways which we recommend. At the same time, the policy which results from such a belief is unlikely to be left in operation unless those who control the press ensure that it behaves with proper restraint and provides its readers with the fair and accurate information and comment essential for responsible judgements. But there is no escape from the truth that a free society which expects responsible conduct must be prepared to tolerate some irresponsibility as part of the price of liberty.

So once again the focus of recommendations was the Press

Council. The Commission started from the premise (par. 20.12) that 'the Council has so far failed to persuade the knowledgeable public that it deals satisfactorily with complaints against newspapers', and suggested that this followed from its attempt to argue (20.15) 'both that it is independent of press interests and that it is a self-regulating body which must therefore maintain a majority of press representatives'. Accordingly the Commission recommended (as had the Younger Committee five years before) that the Council's lay members should be equal in number to its press representation, under an independent chairman who should also preside over the process of choosing them – seeking out (20.24) 'people of quality and reputation'. Although it discounted the idea of a Press Ombudsman, the Commission proposed that the Council should employ a conciliator whose work might speed redress.

The main redress on offer would remain publicized correction. (The Commission could not agree on whether complainants to the Council must still waive their right to sue.) The Council should widen the grounds on which it rebuked newspapers: it should derive from past adjudications a code of behaviour on which to found future ones, be free to censure conduct in breach of the code's spirit as well as its letter, be prepared (20.74) 'to undertake a wider review than it normally does at present of the record of the publication or journalist concerned', investigate press conduct without waiting for a formal complaint, and find grounds for censure in inaccuracy (and contentious opinion based on it) even if later corrected. Besides all this, the Council should increase its own effectiveness by advertising its services, securing a right of reply for people criticized inaccurately, and persuading newspaper publishers' organizations (20.73) 'to agree that their members should undertake to publish adjudications which uphold complaints on the front page of the newspaper in question'.

A brief minority report by David Basnett (leader of the National Union of General and Municipal Workers) and Geoffrey Goodman (industrial editor of the *Daily Mirror*) argued that none of this went far enough. They preferred the National Printing Corporation idea, on the lines of the TUC's suggestion – a subsidiary of the National Enterprise Board which should improve the press's balance by the use of public money. The authors acknowledged that the suggestion was a rough outline only. For the rest, though, the McGregor report was open-mindedly researched (its tables and appendixes offered sustenance to students of the press for years to come), quietist and unalarmist.

Besides improved journalistic behaviour, the Commission's other main desideratum was diversity. The two aims were linked: it was lack of diversity in the coverage of industrial relations which gave rise (along with infractions of privacy by a few national newspapers) to the largest body of significant complaint. Yet diversity of ownership had its importance, too. Among national newspapers, it had not much diminished since the time of the Shawcross report; but concentration had increased among provincial papers, especially weeklies, with 'large geographical groupings' the result (4.21). Although the public interest was not yet suffering, the Commission recommended that the anti-monopoly rules which had resulted from the Shawcross report should be tightened. Those rules provided that a merger between newspapers should proceed unless it was shown to be against the public interest. The Commission proposed the addition of a couple of inhibiting negatives: it should not proceed unless it was shown not to be against the public interest, as gauged from specified guidelines. The circulation limits below which the appointed machinery would cut out should be lowered. Evidence that an existing group was abusing its monopoly should entitle the Government, if so recommended by the Monopolies and Mergers Commission, to oblige the group to shed part of its holding. Cross-holdings between newspaper and broadcasting interests should be in various ways discouraged. Editors should be protected against their employers with twelve-month contracts.

If owners can be enemies of diversity, so can unions. It

161

was a recurrent theme of the report that (17.9) 'for some purposes, the press must be regarded as an industry like any other although, from the point of view of its contribution to the maintenance of democracy, it has to be seen as an industry like none other'. The Commission avoided the question of industrial democracy on newspapers, but following that dictum it took a robust line about print workers who interfered with the press (17.16): 'We think it vital that all who work in newspapers accept as a requirement of citizenship in a democracy that industrial strength should never be used to impede or prevent the publication of information or comment which is disagreeable to a group of workers engaged in the printing of it.' An understood right of reply might help. (There had been a recrudescence of such action at the *Observer* and the *Sun*, in the week before the Commission's report was published, over editorial handling of a dispute at the Grunwick works in north London. Again, though, it was an issue of which the print workers felt that they had special knowledge, since some of their number had picketed the plant.)

But the great question which had arisen since the Commission started work was whether diversity was likely to be inhibited by the National Union of Journalists and its demands for a closed shop. Here the Commission was carefully pragmatic: in general the closed shop was here to stay, events had shown that the law did well to keep out of industrial relations, and yet journalism needed safeguards. So when the Industry Secretary came to draw up the press charter required by the Trade Union and Labour Relations (Amendment) Act, it should include (17.20):

(a) Freedom of a journalist to act, write and speak in accordance with conscience without being inhibited by the threat of expulsion or other disciplinary action by his union or his employer.
(b) Freedom for an editor of a newspaper, news agency or periodical to accept or reject any contribution whether or not the contributor is a professional journalist or a

member of a union, so long as this freedom is not abused.
(c) Freedom for an editor to join or not to join any union
and, if a member of a union, to take part or not to take
part in any industrial action called for by the union.
(d) Protection of an editor's right to accept or reject any
contribution notwithstanding the views of his proprietor, the management of his company, union chapel
or any advertiser or potential advertiser.
(e) Proper appeal procedures for complaints of unfair or
arbitrary expulsion or exclusion from trade union
membership.
(f) Assurance that the practices of publishers and of the
NUJ and IOJ in matters affecting the freedom of journalists will conform with the spirit and provision of the
charter.

Certain of the NUJ's rules should be altered to match this
charter, and the tribunal for dealing with complaints under
it should be the strengthened Press Council. If after three
years an independent committee concluded that a per-
missive system was a failure, then the charter should be
given statutory force. (It was this distant prospect of
legislation, a prospect although distant, which enabled
both right and left on the Commission – except Basnett –
to approve the same scheme.)

The report backed the idea of a single union for print
workers, advocated increased employment of women and
black people among them, and castigated managements
and unions for allowing agreements to be broken in 'suicidal'
fashion. A few justified words were included about the need
for more graduates in journalism, and more graduate
(though not undergraduate) courses for journalists. On
press law, the Commission contented itself with urging the
Government to make up its mind on Franks, Younger,
Phillimore and Faulks. It found itself in general support of
all four, with a few glosses. (These legal deliberations
promised to be endless. In June 1977 Professor Bernard
Williams, a Cambridge philosopher, had been appointed to

163

lead an inquiry into the law of obscenity.)

That aside, little in the report needed State action. New legislation about the press was in any case unlikely, either from the immobilized Callaghan Government or from the Conservative administration which seemed its most probable successor. To lessen the bad behaviour of newspapermen, the country was still to rely on their collective self-discipline, encouraged by a lay eye. It was the wisest decision within reach. Certainly, self-discipline would not root out all faults; but then, nor would discipline from outside, either. The power which imposed it could in the end only be the State's, and the State's tests for good behaviour in the press might well allow attitudes which in terms of the public good were the most damaging faults of all: in-attentiveness or complaisance in observing authority.

Implicitly, this reluctant non-interference rested on a further argument: that though all newspapers would continue to show faults, the faults themselves would differ. One paper would foster one set of prejudices or assumptions; another would honour an opposite set; and at length, out of individual unfairness, collective fairness would emerge. It was the principle of diversity applied politically where Annan had upheld it culturally.

Annan spoke of regulated diversity – regulated, that is, by bodies deriving their power from the State. In broadcasting, with so few channels to be had, even diversity needs organizing, through some such device as an Open Broad-casting Authority; and no one but the State can make the necessary arrangements. But State-organized diversity is wrong for newspapers, for the same reason that State-imposed discipline is wrong: newspapers need owe nothing to the State, nor fear anything from it, and if they do their capacity for reporting it will be inhibited. Diversity in newspapers must grow of itself out of the impulses of diverse individuals and groups.

It is true that not everyone with a distinct point of view can raise the money to give it expression in a newspaper or a television programme. But if you allow the State to supply that lack, and to become in consequence the ultimate licensing authority for newspapers as well as for broadcasting, you forfeit a far more valuable diversity than anything gained in its place. And even the State's coffers are not bottomless: there would be competition for its newspaper funds; it could not bankroll numberless newspapers, nor promise limitless life to those of them which showed no sign of paying their way.

No degree of diversity could be total, however highly engineered. To match the diversity of humankind you would need national newspapers numbered in thousands, broadcast programmes fragmented into tiny time-slots; and then very few people would read or hear any one of them. That is why talk of the citizen's right of access to the media is a fraud. If it existed, it would be self-defeating. His only effective right, when he has first made sure that he has fellow-enthusiasts, is to launch off on his own.

In such a system – haphazard, as all free systems are – the diversity attained can still be representative enough. The launching of many of the types of newspaper at present missing is regularly canvassed and perfectly feasible. There is no reason, for a start, why the State itself should not be one of the new proprietors, if politicians of the Government party felt strongly enough about it. A State-owned newspaper would have clear advantages in the gathering of certain political and foreign news. It would also be able to test the belief, habitual among politicians in power, that there is a far wider market than newspapermen suppose for good news – even if it is only of the type: 'Most factories in the country worked normally yesterday.' On the other hand, a State-owned paper would be inhibited when the news was inescapably bad for the Government, and it would be permanently constrained in its political comment. It would not be excused leader-writing, as broadcasters are: it would have to devise something to fill the leader-column. Its problem would be to be believed as an independent voice; and if public disbelief kept its circulation low, it could not easily adopt the circulation-boosting expedients used by its commercial competitors.

There is no reason why the TUC, again, should not return to newspaper ownership. The members of its constituent unions are much more numerous than they were in the days of the *Daily Herald*, as well as wealthier. Individual unions might similarly make the attempt, aiming wider than their own members. A consortium of the print unions and the NUJ would be especially well placed. A variant of the same idea, and a slightly more promising one, is that a paper should belong not to the unions in the trade as bodies but to the actual workers in the building. If the system could be made to succeed, it would relieve among print workers that sense of non-involvement amounting to alienation which is at the back of the industry's recurrent strife. (Improved ways of consulting them will in any case need devising.) There would be value, finally, in an effective voice among newspapers for many kinds of counter-culture or alternative society, to give currency to such ideas as are undeservedly buried in the underground press.

Any such publications would face great difficulties. Their owners would have to learn, as commercial managements one by one have learnt this century, to leave the editor to edit. Their influence could be no more than the setting of a general tone. Otherwise they would lose both writers and readers. Keeping their readers would be their most crushing problem: the history of British newspapers for nearly two hundred years suggests that these are exactly the kinds of publication which are in danger of being admired but not bought. They could correspond to a real and existing section of opinion, and yet not convert enough of it into a body of paying readers; and income would be inadequate, and service to readers would decline, and circulation and revenue would fall further, and in the end the backers would lose their zest for throwing good money after bad – just as the State would have done, if its money had been engaged.

It is conceivable that this life-and-death power lodged with the reader, and so mercilessly exercised, will be modified by the new technology of printing. Because computer-setting needs less human help than present hot-metal methods, it is cheaper in operation. Fewer readers, in consequence, will suffice a publication which uses it. As against that, the new hardware is expensive to install, and the entire technology is not yet within the reach of any national newspaper. There are still technical problems to be solved; and it is a fair presumption that when they are long settled there will still be human problems, since – particularly in a time of recession – the print unions will remain understandably anxious to protect as many jobs as they can. In June 1977 the *Financial Times*, which two years before had been among the first national newspapers to decide for innovation, announced that it was shelving its plans 'after a careful examination of union attitudes'. The new technology will not be galloping to the aid of the new diversity for a good many years yet. Even when it does, the product will still have to compete for a market. The reader will still be king.

There is a hitch of the same kind in television. The great aid to diversity there is cable, meaning wired (as distinct from wireless) transmission to individual dwellings. Since broadcast frequencies are not used, the only limit on the number of signals which can be brought to a television set is the number of lines that can be packed into a co-axial cable. The choice offered the viewer could be almost too rich for his peace of mind. The one snag is that the cables have to be there, and for the most part they are not. Any national provision would take twenty years and cost unimaginable and unjustifiable sums.

The problem of diversity can expect no magic resolution. The necessary variety of viewpoints – necessary to secure fairness by the rough expedient of setting one unfairness against another – will not be supplied by new organizations, or not on any saving scale. So, since the whole will not be thus diversified, diversity must be found within the parts. Existing newspapers and programmes will have to accommodate new and sometimes unsympathetic voices within their own allowances of space and time. Editors will need to develop a new tolerance of discordant contributions from outside. Newspapers will have to begin writing evaluatively about each other and even themselves.

Many of the problems of national newspapers and broadcasting organizations in Britain proceed from their being few. They are few because they operate in a compact country, and their restricted number is a source of strength to them: it gives them the resources to attempt a comprehensive job. But it has its drawbacks; and they go wider than lack of diversity. If these organizations are few to share the dividends, they are also few to share the responsibility and the blame. Each of them becomes an important channel from Government to governed, and therefore a target for Government persuasion; a large employer of labour, and thus sensitive to urgings from the unions; an extensive commercial enterprise, and inclined as a result to the change-resistant values of the business world; dependent on the good will of a great many readers and listeners and viewers, and hence careful of current social orthodoxy. These are the conflicting forces which draw the media constantly into the ring of political dispute. It is good for journalists that they should be regularly buffeted there. They do a good deal of buffeting themselves; to be knocked about in their turn keeps their biases in check. But they have to resist: if they allowed any single contender to overcome them permanently, they would lose the power to expound each contender to the others, and new ideas to all of them. Journalists must remain masters of their own destiny and controllers of the process of improving their own work, even though they will often betray their destiny and withhold needed improvement. The politics of the media ought not to grow any less turbulent than they have been.

Bibliography

Anthony Smith, ed., *British Broadcasting* and *The British Press Since the War* (both David and Charles, 1974): anthologies from the important documents, with commentary.

The *BBC Handbook* for any year contains a useful list of dates from the beginning of broadcasting, as well as the full text of the BBC's current Charter and of its Licence and Agreement, and the constitution of its Programme Complaints Commission. The IBA's Annual Report and Accounts is less useful, but does carry the IBA's code of Advertising Standards and Practice.

H. Phillip Levy, *The Press Council* (Macmillan, 1967): a lawyer's account of its origins and rulings.

Asa Briggs, *The History of Broadcasting in the United Kingdom* (Oxford University Press, four volumes, 1961, 1965, 1970 and 1978): a history of the BBC from 1922 to the ending of its monopoly in 1954, with an engaging school-magazine quality, mentioning as many names as possible.

H. H. Wilson, *Pressure Group* (Secker and Warburg, 1961): an admirably detailed account of the campaign for commercial television.

Peter Black, *The Mirror in the Corner* (Hutchinson, 1972): a *Daily Mail* television critic's eclectic history of television between 1952 and 1970, more sympathetic than H. H. Wilson to the coming of ITV.

Reginald Bevins, *The Greasy Pole* (Hodder and Stoughton, 1965): valuably indiscreet about the struggles within the Conservative Cabinet over the Television Act 1964.

Lord Thomson of Fleet, *After I Was Sixty* (Hamish Hamilton, 1975): delighted diary of how the *Scotsman*, STV, Kemsley and *Times* deals were done.

Grace Wyndham Goldie, *Facing the Nation: Television and Politics, 1936–76* (Bodley Head, 1977): a demonstration, from a long-service current-affairs producer, of the delicacy the BBC has found it necessary to use in handling politicians.

Colin Seymour-Ure, *The Political Impact of Mass Media* (Constable, 1974): sensible academic reflections on the question of effect, with case studies: one on Parliament and television deals with the Fourteen-Day Rule and the question of broadcasting debates. His *The Press, Politics and the Public* (Methuen, 1968) has a useful chapter on legal restraints.

Charles Wintour, *Pressures on the Press* (André Deutsch, 1972): an editor's view of Fleet Street, including a well-informed account of how the old *Herald* turned into the new *Sun*, a frank chapter on

169

Bibliography

minor advertising pressures, and helpful reminiscences about parliamentary privilege, contempt and libel.

Jonathan Aitken, *Officially Secret* (Weidenfeld and Nicolson, 1971), recounts the origins of the Official Secrets Act and its use in the *Sunday Telegraph* case.

The Thalidomide Children and the Law: A Report by the Sunday Times (André Deutsch, 1973) gathers together the main articles carried by the newspaper and the legal judgements on whether publishing its findings about the drug's origin would be contempt of court. (They finally appeared in the issue of 27 June 1976.)

Hugo Young, *The Crossman Affair* (Hamish Hamilton and Jonathan Cape in association with the *Sunday Times*, 1976), elegantly sets out the political and legal arguments over the Crossman diaries, which the paper serialized, including the Widgery judgement in full.

Ron McKay and Brian Barr, *The Story of the Scottish Daily News* (Canongate, Edinburgh, 1976): a commendably balanced inside account.

A. C. H. Smith, *Paper Voices* (Chatto and Windus, 1975), documents gradations within the popular press in a study of the *Daily Express* and the *Daily Mirror* between 1945 and 1965.

Raymond Williams, *The Long Revolution* (Chatto and Windus, 1961; Pelican, 1965), contains an excellent chapter called 'The Growth of the Popular Press' (from 1665 to 1959). It is more persuaded than this book is of the natural goodness of popular taste.

Graham Cleverley, *The Fleet Street Disaster* (Constable, 1976), presents a management man's case that national newspapers have got their advertising rates all wrong (and their wage structures too, but manning in Fleet Street had begun to change before the book was published). The book also gives a glimpse of the early history of the print unions.

Rex Winsbury, *New Technology and the Press: a study of experience in the United States* (Royal Commission on the Press working paper no. 1, HMSO, 1975), summarizes the new methods for laymen.

Francis Williams, *Dangerous Estate* (Longmans, Green, 1957), provides a compendious history of the British press from 1702 to 1955. The best passage is about the *Herald*'s attempt to win new readers in the 1930s by bribing them. Williams edited the *Herald* from 1936 to 1940.

Phillip Knightley, *The First Casualty: The War Correspondent as Hero, Propagandist and Myth Maker from the Crimea to Vietnam* (André Deutsch, 1975): an important account of one of journalism's worst failures.

Index

Aberfan disaster, 49, 51, 134
access, 58, 165
ACTT, 106
advertising magazines, 44-5
advertising rates, 88-9, 170
Advertising Standards Authority, 94
Advisory Conciliation and Arbitration Service, 100
Aitken, Jonathan, 52, 170
Albert, Prince, 135
Aldermaston march, 34
Alexander, General Henry, 52
Allen, Sir Douglas, 140
American Gas Company, 25
Annan Committee, 13, 66, 151-7, 164
Associated Newspapers, 79
Astor, David, 105; Astor family, 73; Astor, W. W., 74-5
Atlantic Richfield, 79
Attlee, Clement, 22, 30
Attorney-General, 49, 61, 62, 134, 141, 144

Baldwin, Stanley, 19
Barr, Brian, 170
Basnett, David, 160-1, 163
Battle of Britain, 19
BBC: pre-war relations with Government, 12, 18-19; Charter and Licence, 13, 24, 37, 46, 66, 118-19, 154, 169; and Fourteen-Day Rule, 19-20, 27-8, 33; in Beveridge report, 20-1; and establishment of commercial television, 21-7; television news, 27, 30, 34; and broadcasting of Parliament, 31-2, 46; and Suez, 32-3; overseas services, 32, 119; 1950s election coverage, 34; in Pilkington report, 43, 45; wins second channel, 45-6; charged with bias in 1970 election, 53; given Lord Hill

as chairman, 54; and *Yesterday's Men*, 54; complaints machinery, 54-5, 150, 154, 169; and commercial radio, 55-8; local radio, 56-8; governors as owners, 71; no gainer from absence of advertisements, 90-1, 93; unimplicated in press charter row, 111-12; legal subordination to Government, 117-20; punished by Wilson, 123; governors as lay opinion, 130; and diversity, 149; in Annan report, 151-7; handbook, 169; history, 169; tact, 169
Beaverbrook, Lord, 72-3, 74, 81, 103; Beaverbrook newspapers, 75, 157
Belfast Telegraph, 81
Benn, Tony, 65
Berry family, 73, 74
Bevan, Aneurin, 46
Beveridge Committee, 13, 17-22, 37, 151
Bevins, Reginald, 44, 46, 169
Black, Peter, 169
Black Dwarf, 59
Blackstone, Sir William, 131
Booth, Albert, 113
Briggs, Asa (Lord Briggs), 169
British Leyland, 157-8
British Rail, 63
Broadcasting, 26
Broadcasting in the Seventies, 57
broadcasting of Parliament: on television, 31-2, 46-7, 169; on radio, 66-7

Cabinet secrecy, 63-5, 137, 140-2
cable television, 167
Cadbury, George, 75; family, 79
Cairns, Colonel Douglas, 52
Callaghan, James, 64-5, 116, 140, 141, 150, 157; Callaghan Government, 137, 145, 154-5, 164

171

173

175